M000013936

The
Peace
Index

The Peace Index

A Five-Part Framework to Conquer Chaos and Find Fulfillment

JEREMIE KUBICEK

WILEY

Published by John Wiley & Sons, Inc., Hoboken, New Jersey.
Published simultaneously in Canada.

For general information on our other products and services or for technical support, please contact our Customer Care Department within the United States at (800) 762-2974, outside the United States at (317) 572-3993 or fax (317) 572-4002.

Wiley also publishes its books in a variety of electronic formats. Some content that appears in print may not be available in electronic formats. For more information about Wiley products, visit our web site at www.wiley.com.

Library of Congress Cataloging-in-Publication Data:
Names: Kubicek, Jeremie, author.
Title: The peace index : a five-part framework to conquer chaos and find
  fulfillment / Jeremie Kubicek.
Description: Hoboken, New Jersey : John Wiley & Sons, Inc., [2023] |
  Includes bibliographical references and index.
Identifiers: LCCN 2022028738 (print) | LCCN 2022028739 (ebook) | ISBN
  9781119985921 (cloth) | ISBN 9781119985976 (adobe pdf) | ISBN
  9781119985914 (epub)
Subjects: LCSH: Peace of mind. | Peace—Psychological aspects. | Calmness.
Classification: LCC BF637.P3 K83 2023 (print) | LCC BF637.P3 (ebook) |
  DDC 158.1—dc23/eng/20220729
LC record available at https://lccn.loc.gov/2022028738
LC ebook record available at https://lccn.loc.gov/2022028739

Cover Design: Paul McCarthy

SKY10035738_081922

This book is dedicated to my mom,
Kianna Kubicek.
Your laugh is contagious, your smile is constant,
and your peace is infectious.
Thank you for loving and caring for all of us,
all the time. I love you!

Content

Acknowledgments

I am so thankful for the following people who played a crucial role in creating the Peace Index. Without them, there wouldn't be an Index that helps so many people worldwide. I want to show appreciation to:

- Frog Orr-Ewing. I first heard the concept of Peace through Purpose, People, and Place at Latimer Minster when living in London. His sermon inspired conversations and the creation of a tool designed to help people understand their levels of Peace. Frog (yes, that is his name) is a Postdoctoral Teaching Fellow of Mission in the Department of Theology at the University of Winchester. He is full of energy and life, and I am thankful for his influence.

- Steve Cockram. Steve and I began building visual tools together in the summer of 2013 as our families decided to move into a manor house on the outskirts of London. We launched GiANT Worldwide that year with the vision of training liberators to unlock people around the world. That vision is happening. Our work is in over 114 countries at current count, and I am grateful for our work together.

- Dr. Joe Hill. Steve Cockram and I had been expanding the original Peace Index (Purpose, People, Place) to include Physical Health. Still, Joe pushed us to codify the tool to be more rounded by focusing on Personal Health and adding Provision. Thank you, Joe, for your input and challenge.

- GiANT Worldwide. We currently have over 800 guides (coaches and consultants) who use the Peace Index regularly to unlock people and help them be more fruitful and free. Special thanks to all the guides for fighting for the highest possible good of the clients you serve. (If you want to learn how to be certified to do that, head on to www.giantworldwide.com.)

There is a plethora (my ode to Three Amigos there) of people who have contributed to this book by supporting me. I want to thank specifically:

- My wife, Kelly. She allowed me to focus intensely for 30 days while she was building our event center/wedding venue at our family Farmstead.

- My People. Special thanks to my kids (Addison, Will, and Kate) for being fabulous 20-somethings. You make my world so peaceful because you are living in Peace. The same goes for my parents, Mike and Kianna. Thank you for working with Kelly doing manual labor while I was typing away!

- Bronson Taylor. Thank you for running GiANT flawlessly, which allows me to create and be a passionate Connector for the movement.
- Kevin DeShazo. Thanks for running so hard with me on our college athletics work (www.culturewins .com). So excited for OU athletics and the many other schools.
- Tracy Rader. Thank you for working with me on several fronts, from speaking management to an excellent Summit Pack partner to a qualified GiANT HQ member. And friend!
- Kary Oberbrunner. Thank you for being my pace car and pushing me to step into my identity quickly. Kary is amazing.
- Andrea Ediger. Thanks for managing my schedule and fighting hard to help me carve out my writing time and order my world.
- Andrew Robinson and Landon Lynch. Thanks for being amazing friends and for pushing me with your edits and inputs in record time. I am so proud of you both and your influence in this world.
- GiANT Partners. Thanks for partnering with me and for giving feedback and for allowing me to call all of you up to higher levels.

Introduction: The War

Think about the time when you were completely at Peace. How long has it been since you experienced that feeling of freedom?

Real Peace. Most people want it, but it often feels unattainable—especially in the world we experience daily.

What is the opposite of Peace?

The answer is war. Conflict, hostility, or hatred as well. Ultimately, the opposite of Peace is chaotic unrest.

You can see chaos in the socioeconomic strains and geopolitical fractures that have led to a tsunami of global instability. We all know them as we review this partial list:

- Nations at war
- A global pandemic
- Political chaos
- Social unrest

- The climate
- Economic upheaval
- Distrust of people

It's no wonder global stress is so high. A Harris Poll, on behalf of the American Psychology Association, revealed the following:

> *"More adults rated inflation and issues related to the invasion of Ukraine as stressors that are higher than any other issue asked about in the 15-year history of the Stress in America poll. This comes on top of money stress at the highest recorded level since 2015, according to a broader Stress in America poll fielded last month."*[1]

The world is full of chaos, which leads to anxiety, gloom, and unrest.

What Happens When There Is No Peace?

A world of chaos camouflages Peace. In this state it is hard to see anything but turmoil.

---

[1]American Psychological Associate. (2022). Inflation, war push stress to alarming levels at the two-year COVID-19 anniversary. (10 March). https://www.apa.org/news/press/releases/2022/03/inflation-war-stress?msclkid=d1f5818bcd6811ecacee480d8f401484 (accessed 26 April 2022).

The book *Mind of the Athlete* by Dr. Jarrod Spencer[2] talks about the four primary negative emotions people tend to struggle with when there is conflict: anger, depression, hate, and anxiety.

He states, "The stronger the emotions are, the more time you are likely to spend thinking about life experiences that led to your feeling these emotions."

Dr. Spencer goes on to explain the definition of each of these negative emotions:

- Anger is emotional hurt.
- Depression is hurt held inward.
- Hate is feeling threatened by someone or something.
- Anxiety is fear of the unknown.

It makes sense that so many people have globally struggled amidst discord and chaos. Lockdowns, lost jobs, inflation, and war can easily lead to emotional hurt—to anger. This leads people to the edge of their capacity to process change in a healthy way. That edginess leads to volatility. We wear our emotions on our sleeve, get hurt by others, and lash out in anger amidst the external uncertainty.

---

[2]Spencer, J. (2016). *Mind of the Athlete: Clearer Mind, Better Performance*. Self-published.

Long periods of anger and hopelessness lead to depression. Social and other media stoke that anger and cause people to implode or explode with self-medication, isolation, and rage.

We can track hate as a result of being isolated for an extended period and not genuinely understanding others or building relational trust. Therefore, a person can quickly feel hatred for other political parties or personalities or persons in their life associated with those threatening people.

Without internal Peace, there will never be external Peace

Hate must encounter extreme love for it to be broken, and segregation or isolation doesn't help. This hatred tends to lead to the fear of the unknown, and that anxiety can lead to rampant worry, and worry is worthless.

The project of Peace begins within. We must calm the internal unrest. The alternatives are to continue to blame others or justify the actions that support our narrative. You must fight for Peace on the inside.

Negative emotions, self-medicating addictions, and hatred fill the hole we create when we lack peace.

Avoidance

Could this be why so many people are focusing on futuristic escapes?

Will technology bring Peace by allowing us to live an alternative life, so we don't have to face and fix our present lives?

Maybe a life change will bring Peace. We sell our home and buy an RV, save money for that epic trip into orbit so we can see the world from a different perspective.

Avoidance isn't the answer. To conquer chaos and find Peace, we need to understand what Peace is and isn't.

Understanding Peace

There are two types of Peace in our world:

- External Peace
- Internal Peace

External Peace is what most people think about at first blink when they hear the word peace. At a speaking event, I surveyed a group of people by asking them, "What comes to mind when you hear the word 'Peace'?" The overwhelming answer was, "War," and stopping any future wars.

That is so interesting as Peace, by definition, is freedom from disturbance.

How many times have you said, "If I could just have some Peace and quiet around here!" The desire for freedom from being disturbed is a goal for many of us. And yet, most don't know how to find that because this level of Peace only occurs internally.

How do you find internal Peace with such a lack of external Peace? This book answers that question. I want to help you conquer the chaos that creates turmoil and improve your Peace Index. The tools you are about to experience will help you win the inner war for your own well-being.

The word "Peace" contains numerous meanings. Phrases, symbols, and shared meanings make it less understood but still desirable. Symbols of Peace include:

Other examples from art, culture, and literature include:

- *War and Peace* by Leo Tolstoy.
- "Peace Train" by Cat Stevens.
- Peace like a river.
- Peace talks.
- Peace pipes.
- "Keeping the Peace."
- Waging Peace.
- Peace signs.
- Peace out.
- Peace, hope, and love.
- Peace of mind, etc.

And one of the most potent phrases on Peace comes from Jesus of Nazareth, "Peace I leave with you. My Peace I give to you. I do not give to you as the world gives. Don't let your heart be troubled or fearful." (John 14:27 CSB)

Almost everyone has wanted world Peace—from activists to prayer warriors to pageant contestants sharing their heart's desires.

The idea of R.I.P.—Rest in Peace—at funerals is the hope that the deceased can finally be free of the chaos and turmoil in this world. RIP is kind of a way of "throwing up our hands" and saying, "Well, if it can't be had in life, then at least there's one place where peace is guaranteed."

Internal Peace

"Never be in a hurry; do everything quietly and in a calm spirit. Do not lose your inner Peace for anything whatsoever, even if your whole world seems upset."
– Saint Francis de Sales

External Peace is a state or period in which there is no war, or a war has ended. Internal Peace is when you experience calm in the mind, body, and spirit. You have become free from anxiety, worry, and drama.

Internal Peace is not the absence of conflict but the ability to handle issues in a way that makes you better, not worse.

Finding Peace of mind amidst chaos results in fewer worries, fears, and anxieties. Inner Peace has some fantastic benefits:

- Better sleep.
- Less drama with friends, coworkers, or family.
- Security, confidence, humility.
- Negatives not sticking to you.
- Resolve amidst trials.
- Increased energy levels and improved emotional management.

> *A person at war with themselves is at war with the world.*

More external unrest calls for more inner Peace!

War with yourself leads to more struggle. Inner Peace brings tranquility irrespective of the external challenges. Some of you may think this is unrealistic. What follows will not only challenge your skepticism, but it may also even make you a believer. I don't believe that we can experience absolute Peace. Our experience of Peace fluctuates like a thermometer. Some seasons offer more Peace than others. The questions we each need to face are: 1) What is my relative sense of Peace at this moment? and 2) How can I increase my sense of Peace tomorrow?

Dealing with the Crazies

The external chaos may not have anything to do with things happening in the world around you. Your external issues may come from your crazy relative, who drives you insane every week. Or your external unrest could be from your teammate at work who behaves erratically or spews negative thoughts about everything daily.

The crazies might be making you crazy. The People in your life could be the ones causing your Peace Index to dip.

Can you be at Peace in a chaotic world? Can you be at ease when you have crazies in your daily life? Can you create an inner Peace when there is no outer Peace?

Can you create Peace when you are the crazy one?

You must choose to create an inner Peace when there is no outer Peace.

Choosing Peace

Inner Peace occurs when you are calm and at ease while irritants, annoyances, and stressors are all around you. Peace of mind happens when you can experience contentment, joy, and bliss when difficult things are happening in your life.

This book helps you find Peace by controlling the controllable moments of life. You'll find the tools you need to select Peace amidst unrest, quiet confidence over chaos, and contentment when there is little reason to be contented.

The path toward Peace begins when you identify the barriers between you and Peace. You'll identify these barriers and how to overcome them. You will learn how to experience Peace when:

- Your Purpose is off, and your future looks grim.
- Your People drive you crazy.
- Your Place is less than ideal.
- Your Personal Health falters.
- Your lack of Provision keeps you awake wondering how you'll pay the bills.

I find the Isaac Wheadon song, "I'm at Peace While the World Isn't," mesmerizing and cathartic. The lyrics repeat over and over:

"It's so amazing / I'm at Peace while the world isn't / I'm at Peace while the world isn't"

What if you were the most peaceful person in the room tomorrow? This book will help you find out what is causing you drama and how to deal with it. It is designed to help you increase the Peace in your life and fight to cultivate your own sense of well-being. You will learn to improve issues by assessing the pain and creating a plan to resolve it.

But you must make a choice. Choosing Peace is just one option. To experience it, you have to choose it.

Doing the Hard Work

A few years ago, my dad took my son and me on an epic Alaska fishing adventure. One day, we were flying on a seaplane that took us deep into the Alaskan wilderness. We caught fish, took terrific pictures, and were chased by a bear (yep, it happened). I didn't want to talk to anyone on the flight back. I was cold and just wanted to warm up and maybe take a catnap.

Just then, I was nudged on the leg by this guy in front of me who slid his earphones off and asked, "What do you do?" I thought, "Really, man, I just want to rest." So, I made up something like, I unlock people and help free them to be themselves.

He told me that he was the CEO of a large company in California and that he had been watching my interactions with my son and dad and was curious to learn more about me. He stated that he saw a Peace in me that he didn't have. We exchanged information, and a week later,

I connected him to two of our GiANT consultants, Jeff Ridenour and Maria Guy.

This CEO knew he had a problem and his issues pushed him to do the hard work.

Success can't coexist with unrest.

Over the next few months, Maria and Jeff began working on the internal unrest occurring in his business. Communication was low, and the relational trust was not strong. This leader needed Peace, and he was willing to do what it took to succeed, which occurred because of his commitment and Maria and Jeff's expertise.

Naming the Unrest

Peace is hard to achieve. Are you willing to do what needs to happen to find Peace and success in your life? How much do you want to conquer the chaos?

If you don't define success for yourself, someone else will. There is a direct correlation to Peace when expectations are realized. The same is true with unrest. If you are not clear on what winning looks like, you may find yourself feeling flustered when you don't meet the expectations you didn't share with others but hold dearly.

It's time to look firmly at any unrest in your life, taking control of the conflict and creating a plan to alleviate it. It's time to find your number so that you can go to work on the right things in the right way to improve your Peace and conquer the chaos.

CHAPTER ONE

The Number over Your Head

Imagine sitting at your favorite coffee shop and watching people stroll in with a number over their head—like a character in a video game. The number hovers in a circle with either green, yellow, or red numbers depending on the person's sense of Peace. Some people had a green 85% over their head, some a powerfully positive green 92%, while others have a warning yellow number of 62.5% or worse; a guy walks in with a red-hot colored 40%.

Imagine the numbers figuratively represent how each person is doing at that moment of the day.

In reality, you don't see a number over people's heads, but you know it's there. You can probably guess the number of each member of your family without much effort. People, including you and me, have numbers telling us how at Peace we are or aren't, and those numbers change every day based on five areas of life. We can go from an 85% on

Monday to a 58% on Wednesday back to a solid 90% by the weekend. Why? Well, that is what this book is about— helping you learn to understand those factors and move them for yourself into healthy green levels.

That is exactly what the Peace Index, the primary tool of this book, will help you do. It will help you assess your level of Peace and the corresponding categories of unrest.

The Reason "How are you?" Doesn't Work

Virtually every day of my life, I have the same short meaningless conversation with numerous people. I say to Amy at the coffee shop, "Good morning, how are you?" And she may respond, "Good, you?" To which I say, "Great, thanks. Have a good day!"

The truth may have been that Amy was at a 71% (out of 100%) that day because her friend shared some frustrating news about another friend. And me? I may have started my day at an 80% until I received some frustrating information about one of my businesses and I dropped to a 68%.

Our lives fluctuate like the stock market. Outside forces drive our Peace Index up or down. For some of us, we are controlled by our feelings to such a degree that our daily % can feel like a roller coaster, which is an indicator of the chaos in our life. Or the Peace.

Dealing with Reality

Years ago, I was off, and I knew it. I couldn't seem to get my bearings. My purpose was off, my view of the future was gone, and I was getting frustrated by the pettiest things. I knew I was off, but I couldn't figure out why. There were several mornings where I woke up in tears, which is not me.

My wife became nervous when she noticed I was watching the same movie for the sixth time in three months. It's true, I watched *We Were Soldiers* starring Mel Gibson, six times over five months.

While I knew I was off, I didn't have the language or the tools to help me solve my issues. I had to deal with my reality, and I began meeting with a coach to help me make it through the most difficult time in my life—the loss of my purpose.

Getting healthy means getting real. We must run toward the issues, not away from them if we plan to solve and deal with them appropriately.

The Number

What is your number? Let's calculate it.

You just need to complete the Peace Index below, which will take you on a journey to learn how to improve your Peace.

It is simple but profound. If you use it regularly, the number over your head goes up because you begin to think about the areas that need improvement more intentionally than you did before. You'll find it helps you formulate specific strategies you can use to improve it. This may sound overly simple, but it is that easy.

There are five segments to the Peace Index. Each circle has a number from 1 to 100% regarding Purpose, People, Place, Personal Health, and Provision. Each of them affects our lives powerfully. Some of them are more important than others to you.

The Peace Index is a tool that allows you to determine your level of Peace. Your notion of Peace may vary greatly from someone else's. For instance, one person's 79% could be another person's 89%. That doesn't matter, as you are likely to be consistent in setting your own % numbers.

Combine each segment (Purpose, People, Place, Personal Health, Provision) to determine your Peace Index. Having completed the index, you'll immediately recognize where you're doing well and the areas that need improvement. When you aggregate all five and divide by five, you will get your Peace Index. We carry this number wherever we go—in coffee shops, airplanes, offices, and shopping. Some people wear their Peace

Index on their sleeves, while others can hide things extraordinarily well.

Complete the Peace Index to assess your current level of Peace. I want you to evaluate yourself at the beginning of the book and then test yourself again at the end after you have analyzed yourself in every circle and created a game plan for growth. Your number will change by the end and establish an excellent baseline for the future.

Let's take a preliminary evaluation here.

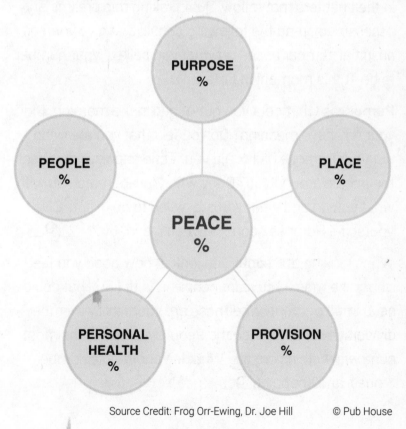

Source Credit: Frog Orr-Ewing, Dr. Joe Hill   © Pub House

The steps are simple: give yourself a number from 1 to 100% in each circle, with 100% being the highest. You can give yourself a 72.5% or whatever you believe is valid for each category. Keep in mind that your numbers could be lower or higher than someone else's. It is like ranking movies. One person's 70% could be someone else's 80%. That doesn't matter. But it is essential that you are honest with yourself on each category.

We will be going through each of these at a deeper level in the chapters that follow. But in taking this preliminary assessment, read the following details and give yourself an initial number based on what you believe your number to be at this moment in time.

Purpose is what gets you out of bed in the morning. Did your day have meaning? Do you feel that you are living out your Purpose daily? Did your actions positively affect the people around you? Does who you are match up with what you do and what you are called to do in life? Give yourself a Purpose score between 1 and100%. __90__

When looking at **People**, you look at how good you feel about the most important people in your life. That could be 5 or 10 or 25 People. These are your family members, coworkers, and friends—the People you spend the most time with within your life. What is your People number from 1 to 100%? __85__

Moving to **Place**, what is your level of Peace related to your spaces: house, neighborhood, town, city, or region? And how do you feel about your workspace or office? All these areas combined summarize your Peace level related to Place. What is your Place number from 1 to 100%? __95__

When you think of **Personal Health**, you might naturally think about your physical health. Physical is one-third of what I mean by Personal Health. Mind, body, and spirit make up your total Personal Health, so where are you when you think of your mental, physical, and spiritual health from 1 to 100%? __90__

Lastly, what is your Peace level as it relates to **Provision**? By Provision, I mean the resources you have available to live your life and do what you desire. Provision is your salary and overall earnings. Most people would gladly accept a raise. That's not what I am talking about. The issue is whether your lack of income keeps you up at night. How well do you feel about your Provision from 1 to100%? __90__

Now, add up all of the numbers and divide the total by five. This will give you your Peace Index in real time. As we go through each chapter you will notice your Peace Index change, most likely improving. Until then, this will provide you the number over your head right now. _90_

When to Measure

"So, how often can I do this?" you ask. My answer is, "Yes."

You can take the Peace Index as many times as you want. I know some people who calendar a quarterly retreat to walk through the Peace Index for themselves and share it with those close to them. Some people calculate their Peace Index three times in a single week if they are in a difficult spot.

The key is to measure and understand that the Peace Index opens the door to self-awareness, and as my friend and business partner Steve Cockram likes to say, "You never graduate from the school of self-awareness."

Measure away, friends. It will just make you better.

You Can't Give What You Don't Possess

Because the Peace Index is about health, you can see where you are healthy and where you are not. When you are not healthy, you may negatively affect someone else's Peace Index. Did you get that? If you are significantly off with your Purpose, you might be causing someone else's People number to be lower because they are trying to help you.

In other words, people don't just *recognize* your Peace Index, they are often *affected* by it. Life is a series of cause and effect. There are ramifications of our actions: consequences. When you are not at your best, you have very little to give to others.

Conversely, you can give what you possess. Those who experience Peace help others experience it, too. It is the best contagion of all. But to give Peace to others, you first need to cultivate it in yourself.

This anonymous quote says it best: "When things change inside you, things change around you."

Intentional Living Has Great Rewards

After going through the Peace issues I mentioned early, I decided to flip my life to become more intentional, specifically as a husband and dad. That meant that I began controlling my emotions instead of letting them control me. I started working on discretion and discipline in managing my work, relationships, and health. People noticed.

I realized that I was focused in certain areas and accidental in other areas. The accidental decisions began to creep into the focused areas, and I suffered the consequences. I will never forget the day I was sitting in my office in Atlanta when I began to experience some physical issues caused by stress. I was CEO of the companies over John Maxwell's training businesses, the Catalyst Conferences, and the Chick-fil-A Leadercast. We worked so hard to make these businesses thrive, which they did. While I was focused intently on my Purpose, I gave little attention to my Personal Health, and the stress of it began to affect the health of the other.

My Peace Index lacked balance. My over-focus on one circle (Purpose) and lack of focus on another (Personal Health) began to affect my Purpose. At the same time, I didn't realize that I was taking my People for granted. I was losing while winning. It took an MRI, which revealed stress-related ailments, and an amazing grace-filled wife to help me slow down enough to see what accidental living was producing.

I began to slow down to speed up. I started to refocus on a bigger Purpose, authentic relationships, and focus on my health (mental, physical, and spiritual). It impacted me so much that I eventually found a replacement to take on my CEO role while transitioning to our current business, GiANT Worldwide. We also moved to London, where we began to live again.

I began to hope again. My Purpose got dusted off as well. While in Atlanta I had allowed my Peace Index to drop to an overall 65%. The change of role and Place affected everything. I had to choose Peace and fight for my higher good to experience it.

How about you? Is it time for a reset of your Peace level?

Is your hope covered up with fear, worry, or despair?

The Hope Meter

Hope is crucial for Peace to exist. It is the belief that our future can be better than our past.

I will never forget when I knew my oldest daughter, Addison, needed some hope. We were driving and I was asking my normal check-in questions. As I took her through the Peace Index, it was evident that her number was very low and needed a boost.

That is where my daughter Addison and I created the tool you are about to learn—the Hope Meter.

I asked her a simple question. "On a scale of 1 to 100%, how well do you feel today about your future (your tomorrow)?"

In my daughter's case, she couldn't see the future very well because of some issues with her Peace Index. That caused a bit of concern, so much so that we used a pen and paper to create this Hope Meter tool:

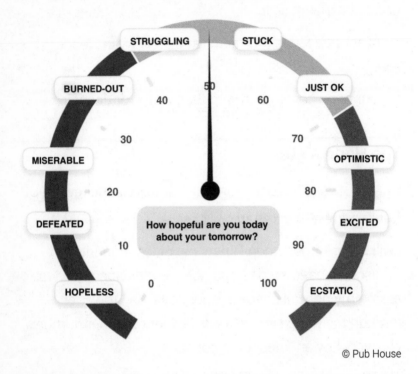

© Pub House

When Steve Cockram and I began creating many of the tools you will use in this book, we started with the concept that they need to be written for an educated 13-year-old to have the best chance of scaling inside organizations and families. My daughter was much older at the time, but the premise still stands—create a visual tool with a common language to allow people to respond to it for their Personal Health and to teach other people.

While I don't remember the actual number Addison gave me that night, I do remember that her number went up dramatically after we discussed it. We identified the pain and frustration and created a plan to address the issue. She realized that a People issue on the Peace Index had been so consistent and had caused her to catastrophize the future so much so that her hope began to fall dramatically.

Hope is the desire for certain things to happen. Hopelessness is rampant in our world. It is the feeling of despair that what you want to happen won't occur. Hopelessness over the long term leads to a depressed spirit, which is like being covered by layer after layer of disappointment and sadness.

What is your Hope Meter in this season of your life?

As I write this today, I am in the high 80s on the Hope Meter. I am optimistic about the future. I am not in the 90s, mainly because I was asked to write this book in 30 days and am in the middle of it. I believe my Hope Meter will climb significantly as I get excited for its release and for you to be impacted by it and give copies of it to other people, encouraging them immensely.

If you want to develop hope in others, use the Hope Meter to ask them where they are and walk them through the Peace Index to create a game plan to improve.

Back to the Number

Just like the Peace Index, we all have a Hope Meter. However, the Peace Index is a more holistic number that can lead to solutions.

A high Peace Index gives you more hope, allowing you to think more clearly about the future. You view the obstacles as challenges instead of barriers when your Peace Index is higher. A person with a higher Peace Index is more secure, confident, and humble. They can bring their best to others because they are healthy, as we discussed, and will tend to empower others more willingly.

Someone with a lower Peace Index is too absorbed with their issues to lead others well. It is hard to bring their best self to others because of their lack of health, and it can undermine their influence and disrupt others very easily.

The Peace Index is a self-evaluation of a person's feelings regarding their current reality. We will dive into each segment in the following chapters and see why one is higher than the other. We will address the one that tends to drive you and the one that tends to be the constant issue.

In the end, I will help you build a game plan to make that segment better so you can work to control the controllable, where possible.

Your Peace Index number is a number that shares your life. You will need someone you trust to help you process your number because some people tend to list your number too low, while others may tend to overstate their health. You each know who you are. Let's agree to work together to get healthy. Deal?

Now, let's dive into the first circle, Purpose, so that you can begin to experience a higher level of growth.

CHAPTER TWO

Purpose: The Reason You Get out of Bed

As I was writing this chapter, I paused for a few hours for some regularly scheduled coaching sessions. The topic for this specific executive was her lack of Purpose. I couldn't believe it. It was perfect timing as I had been researching Purpose for weeks.

My client has worked as a sales executive for the past 17 years but feels trapped in her current role. She is friends with her company's founder but believes that her skills are much higher than her position. The problem is that she has spent her years helping this entrepreneur fulfill his dreams but doesn't have a vision for herself. She has lost her passion and can't see the vision for her life. Her current dream feels more like a nightmare at times, and she knows she can't continue to fake it.

She aligned her job title and position so close to her Purpose that her identity would be negatively affected if she were to leave. Therefore, she thinks she will lose momentum if she chooses a better Peace. I showed her that she had already lost the internal momentum—her Purpose.

This identity issue happens frequently. I have coached executives in globally respected businesses who have worked over 20 years in the company and realized that their Purpose became grafted into the company.

I have seen this happen within strong company cultures as well as those who have strong loyalties to the founders. I have met with several owner–operators of the successful Chick-fil-A organization who have worked 25+ years only to find that they had lost their personal vision as it became trumped by the company's vision.

The company's Purpose became theirs. That means that their identity became a VP of this or Director of that or President of whatever. The title, the organization's mission, and vision took over their identity. These people, therefore, have a difficult time imagining what life would look like without their status. It is hard to move on or leave because they don't know what to do afterward. If they leave, they lose their Purpose.

Because they are grafted in, they lose hope with the fear that their best lives—their reason for being—are behind them. That can be depressing.

Does this sound pertinent to any one of you?

Purpose Versus Responsibility

What gets you out of bed in the morning? I know, I know—an alarm. Other than that, why do you do what you do?

"I don't know," some could say, "I just do what I am supposed to do."

"Supposed to do" is not a Purpose. Nor is "responsibilities." Those come after Purpose. They don't define it.

> *Purpose is the central motivating aim of your life—the reason you get up in the morning.*

Purpose can guide life decisions, influence behavior, shape goals, offer a sense of direction, and create meaning. For most, Purpose is connected to vocation— what you do. I like to think that Purpose mixes who you are with what you do.

Purpose is more "want to" than "have to." Are you getting out of bed every morning because you "have to" or "want to"? "I have to take the kids to school." "I have to go to work to make money to pay for the mortgage and the car and the braces and the. . ." Is your Purpose tied to your responsibilities as a parent, employee, or boss? Or does your Purpose come from the core of your existence and the meaning of your life?

Purpose mixes who you are with what you do.

If "have to" is the norm, it is time to dust off your vision and work toward what you want. It might just be time to reflect on why you were born, what skills you bring to the world, and how you can fulfill your God-given talent.

The Golden Years

You have time to figure out your Purpose. As I share stories, I don't want to cause despair, but, rather, provide perspective.

To help the executive I mentioned at the start of this chapter, I took her through an exercise I tend to use to frame the perspective of her Purpose. Why don't you join me by following this exercise as well?

For years, I have been studying the typical ages of leaders in critical roles, industries, and countries. I have discovered that the most influential years in a leader's life are between 55 and 70 years old. "What!" most will exclaim (especially the young bucks). I know that sounds preposterous but hear me out.

The average age of the president of the United States at the time of inauguration is 55.

The average age of CEOs is 59.

The average age of a U.S. congressperson is 57.

The average age of a U.S. senator is 63.

The average age of university presidents is 62.

I once had a chance to speak to the mayors of every prominent city in Germany at a hidden restaurant under the German embassy in Brussels. We were all gathered around with Munich-style drinks, the predictable giant pretzel, and some of the best schnitzel I have ever had. I inquired about their ages and averaged them together. Want to guess what it was? Fifty-nine years old.

The prominent positions in the world are led by those aged 55 to 70. Why is that? Precisely because they have:

- Focused on a Purpose that fits them.
- Failed and succeeded repeatedly.
- Time to focus on their Purpose as they have finally sent off those pesky kids (sort of joking).
- Money to do what they want to do.
- Influence because of their competencies and years of credibility.
- Connections with other influencers who help them with their Purpose.

What does that mean for you and your Purpose?

It means that you have time to prepare for your Purpose.

The exercise is simple. Subtract your current age from 55. The answer is how many years you have before entering your influence years. I have five. What about you? Some may have 10 years, and some may say 22 years. I also realize that some may be two years into their influence years or even more. That is perfect. It is never too late to step into your Purpose.

The sales executive I was coaching realized that there was time. She wasn't late. She could still live out her purpose even though she was frustrated for staying too long in a job that now caused her despair.

I find that most people feel relieved when they go through this exercise. It gives perspective. It helps you realize that you are in a marathon, not a sprint. You can shift your mind to prepare for the influence seasons. I find that Peace often improves on this idea alone. Marinate on this big idea—you have time to figure out your Purpose. You don't have to hurry—you can rest in hope. You can find what you were designed to do.

Calling

Of the five P words in the Peace Index, Purpose is the most important for me. It is my leading indicator, my driver. If it is off, everything else in my life is off. I must know that what I am doing matters. For others it may be People, Personal Health, or another of the P words.

Another way to describe Purpose is what I am called to do. What do I have a strong urge to do with my vocation—like a conviction? That is the level of Purpose that I have always desired.

It means that at the end of my life, I have lived out my Purpose and done what I was called to do.

My wife knew that she wanted to be a dental hygienist in kindergarten. Sure enough, she became a dental hygienist. We then had children, and her Purpose changed. She felt called to make her work the raising of our kids. That was a good, long season. However, her Purpose was not tied solely to our children. She did the hard job of dusting off her vision and Purpose. She started a company called Visionary and is now a developer of neighborhoods, event spaces, and homes.

Do you know what you were made to do?

Do you fully grasp what you are naturally gifted to do?

Do you know what you are passionate about doing?

Purpose is an ongoing journey, and callings change with the seasons.

All of us have a Purpose; some find it.

Activating Purpose

While traveling through Asia in college, I learned a Japanese concept called *ikigai*. This philosophy stands for your "reason for being." *Iki* means life, and *gai* means value or worth. Simply, it means your life's worth, or even better, your life purpose—the inspiration that gets you out of bed in the morning.

That trip led me to study this age-old concept of understanding Purpose. Many of you have seen this diagram but may not know its origin. I have used it for decades to help people see something deeper inside of them.

I like how the process causes you to think about your Purpose. The concept focuses on:

- What you love.
- What you're good at.
- What you can be paid for.
- What the world needs.

Ikigai can be a mirror as you consider your future, especially if you feel stuck in your current season. Use this list of questions as an assessment to help you move more intentionally into your life's purpose.[1] You can assess yourself by giving a score (1 to 5, with 5 being the highest) for each question. I have listed my scores below:

1. What you love: (1 to 5)
   a. Do your passions match with your line of work?   5
   b. Is your daily work satisfying and motivating?   3.5
   c. Can other people see that in you?   4

---

[1]This list is a modified version of the list found at https://www. betterup.com/blog/what-is-ikigai.

2. What you are good at: (1 to 5)

   a. Do you have influence with your colleagues regarding your work? 4

   b. Do you feel that your work fits into your conscious competence? 5

   c. Would you be considered an expert in your work? 4.5

3. What you can be paid for: (1 to 5)

   a. Is your sector or industry growing? 5

   b. Is your specific expertise in demand? 4

   c. Are people willing to pay you what you are worth? 4

4. What you believe the world needs: (1 to 5)

   a. Will your work be valuable over the next 25+ years? 5

   b. Are you solving problems that help people? 5

   c. Is your work or business in high demand? 4

My score is 53 out of 60 (88%). I feel as if I am in a higher season at this stage of life. I have been a lot lower and possibly a bit higher as well.

Your turn. Take the assessment to get to a reality about your Purpose.

1. What you love: (1 to 5)

   a. Do your passions match with your line of work? _____

   b. Is your daily work satisfying and motivating? _____

   c. Can other people see that in you? _____

2. What you are good at: (1 to 5)

   a. Do you have influence with your colleagues regarding your work? _____

   b. Do you feel that your work fits into your conscious competence? _____

   c. Would you be considered an expert in your work? _____

3. What you can be paid for: (1 to 5)

   a. Is your sector or industry growing _____?

   b. Is your specific expertise in demand _____?

   c. Are people willing to pay you what you are worth _____?

4. What you believe the world needs: (1 to 5)

   a. Will your work be valuable over the next 25+ years _____?

   b. Are you solving problems that helps people _____?

   c. Is your work or business in high demand _____?

The minimum score possible is 12 and the maximum score possible is 60. Answer each question with a number, 1 to 5, for each and tally the numbers for your total score.

The ikigai is one example of answering questions to help you strengthen your Purpose.

Purpose Number

Purpose in the Peace Index is focused on how good you feel about what you are designed to do.

- How clear is your sense of meaning, direction, and fulfillment in life?
- Is your work satisfying?
- Does it bring out your skills and allow you to use your superpowers?
- How fulfilled are you with the job you are doing?

After pondering Purpose, what number, 1 to 100% (100% as the highest), would you now give yourself for Purpose?

My Peace Index number acts as an indicator for when it might be time to do a deep dive into where my Purpose might be unclear or misaligned. Sometimes I realize something is off and needs adjustment. Other times I find I am right where I need to be and just need to remember the significance of my work when I have started going through the motions.

Knowing Yourself

All of us have a Purpose; some of us find it. The goal is to understand yourself so well that you can lead yourself through the process of finding the meaning of getting out of bed in the morning.

Each of us has these superpowers that are God-given. Some of us are incredible helpers; others are builders; some are highly logical, while others can carry rooms with enthusiasm. We are all made differently for the benefit of the whole. It is a grand design to keep balance and work within the masses.

Some of us enjoy the organization we work with but may not love the role we play now, which can affect our Purpose.

Steve Cockram created a tool called 70/30 that helps people see what part of their current role they feel good about and what are the less than fulfilling areas.

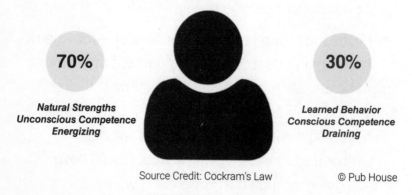

70%

Natural Strengths
Unconscious Competence
Energizing

30%

Learned Behavior
Conscious Competence
Draining

Source Credit: Cockram's Law   © Pub House

The ideal work level would be 70% of your time working in your sweet spot—those areas of natural strength, energizing as you do what you are excellent at doing. The other 30% would be the activities you can do but don't necessarily love. These things may be draining as you have learned how to do them, but they are not your sweet spot.

Just like the Peace Index, your 70/30 can change often. It can move to 60/40, 50/50, or fall below the line to 40/60 or worse, 30/70. It is a reality that you will drown if you are underwater too long. You can hold your breath for a while, but your Peace Index will most likely fall if your work is under 50/50 for too long.

On the other side, it can be good to get to 80/20, but if you get to 90/10, you might have a little narcissism as you might need to take out the trash a bit. The ideal is 70/30.

I have spent much of my career as a CEO around 50/50. This tool helped me immensely as I started to list my 70 and 30 and began delegating certain items and taking on others. So, let's do that here.

Your 70%: What areas in your work and or life would you say are natural strengths that energize you when you do them and make you feel that you are unconsciously competent at doing?

- help others
- Organize
- keep Calendars
- multi-task
- Complete task w/sense of urgency

Your 30%: On the other side, what parts of your work are you doing that, while you have learned to do, drain you? These are areas you would like to do less of in your job.

- *be patient and wait on Others*
- *last minute "on fire" requests*
- *Creativity on the spot*
- _____
- _____

The more secure and confident your Purpose is, the more helpful you are to those in your life and work. The more you can get into your 70% sweet spot, the more you will thrive.

My goal is to help you deal with your insecurities, frustrations, or fears. I want to help you see the areas that are off related to your Peace. That is how we work toward increasing the Peace Index.

I love how J. Donald Walters states it:

> *"You will find Peace not by trying to escape your problems, but by confronting them courageously. You will find Peace, not in denial but victory."*

Who Says We Can't?

I remember meeting an aristocratic landowner while sitting in the famed Cliveden House when I was writing *The 5 Gears*. I would run into him almost daily as

I spent a few hours a day in their renovated riding stables-turned-cafe doing my work. My friend was fascinated by who I was and what I was doing in this region of England. "Jeremie," he said, "tell me about your family. What is your history?" I would then tell him that I grew up in a farming family and how my family moved from Prague, Czechoslovakia, to Prague, Oklahoma, to farm. I shared that we had rented a 10-bedroom manor house across from his thousands of acres. He would chuckle as we had this consistent conversation.

The realities are that I didn't go to Eton (a famed school in England) or an Ivy League university. My family heritage is farming, and our farm in Econtuchka, Oklahoma, is over 100 years old, which is one of the reasons we moved from London back to Oklahoma.

One of the attributes of Oklahoma is that it is filled full of pioneers who share the attitude of "Who says we can't?!" If you can make it in Oklahoma, you can make it anywhere, especially when you study the historical hardships of this land.

I liked the concept so much that we created a visual tool to help people step into their Purpose. It is fittingly called, Who Says You Can't?

I started saying this to myself when I was 21 years old, starting companies in Moscow with my business partners. It was a constant refrain as I traveled back and forth to the United States, merging businesses for our distribution company. The same thinking happened when we launched a global simulcast, moved to London, built a neighborhood, and started launching scalable SaaS (subscription model) tech companies.

There is a strange dilemma with most people I have helped, including myself. Most people have limiting beliefs. While living in Atlanta, I experienced interesting social dynamics in the South tied to family history. I would often hear, "So, what does your family do?" It was as if success came from family heritage. I experienced this to the extreme while living in London. "Tell me about your family" meant quite a lot as family heritage was tied to a caste-like system around heritage, schooling, and occupation.

INHIBITION   *or*   # PROHIBITION

*Limiting
Beliefs*

*Enforced
Restrictions*

© Pub House

Who says you can't? asks you if your desire to accomplish something has any 1) inhibition, which is limiting beliefs, or 2) prohibition, which are enforced restrictions.

Most people don't think they are allowed to do certain things—thinking they are prohibited. The reality is that most people are inhibited. The limiting beliefs inside them keep them from ever experiencing true Peace.

One of our GiANT consultants, Jay Sampson, shared this story about one of his clients that highlights this point.

> As I met with a client with a team of three, some fatigue was pretty apparent. As they took the Peace Index, I was surprised to hear the totals of 62%, 55%, and 43%, respectively. As we dove into the numbers, one of the participants knew that her People category was low but couldn't comprehend how Purpose had gotten so low.
>
> One of the participants was doing AR / AP for a medical company and had moved from Arizona to Oklahoma to avoid a toxic relationship. She is a certified Holistic Nutritionist doing financial work, and while she is good at it, it isn't her Purpose. As we dug in deeper, we identified the resistance which was inhibiting her—she needed more certifications to perform specific procedures. I kept asking her why those facts meant she couldn't do the work she enjoyed since she knew what she needed to do to get certified. We finished that meeting and scheduled the next one.

At the start of the next meeting, she said (and I quote), "I felt like last time, you were telling me to get my act together. So, I did some research. And I don't have to have a four-year degree to do some of the work. I need a two-year degree. And I already have most of that completed. Also, I thought it through, and I could take on some clients on the weekend—I have time—and generate some extra income that would be very helpful. AND I can continue doing a job that is easy for me because I am good at it and working with a team that I enjoy." I realized that most of my clients need a sounding board to help them see what is right in front of them.

What are the limiting beliefs keeping you from stepping into your true Purpose? Wouldn't that be silly if a petty fear kept us from really doing what we are designed to do?

So, when you get out of bed in the morning ask yourself: "What was I designed to do today? How can I live out my Purpose today?"

When we step into our Purpose—the mix of who we are with what we do—we will find more profound levels of Peace. We need people who care for us to help us—to call us up and not out. The next chapter will show us how healthy our People levels are and how we can make them better.

CHAPTER THREE

People: Those Who Make Us or Break Us

There are people you have to love, people you want to love, and people you get to love. At the same time, there are people you must work with, people you want to work with, and people who you simply pass by every day.

Who are the ones who love you, who push you to higher levels while quite possibly also pushing your buttons?

An anthropologist named Robin Dunbar developed something called Dunbar's Number. The premise proposes that humans can comfortably maintain up to 150 stable relationships. While many people have argued his findings, I think it is interesting how he describe relationships as "the number of people you would not feel embarrassed about joining uninvited for a drink if you happened to bump into them in a bar."[1]

His definition of a stable relationship is one where you are not embarrassed by the other person.

How People Affect You

You have heard it said, "People, you can't live with them, and you can't live without them." That is so true. My favorite all-time band, U2, said it this way in the song "With or Without You":

"With or without you / With or without you, oh / I can't live / With or without you"

People are a paradox. We need them, and yet they can drive us crazy.

The actions of others cause a reaction from you. It is often the little things that get under your skin or cause you great joy over time. Here is a list of petty actions. How do they affect you?

- How do you feel when someone is scrolling on their phone while you are talking to them?
- What is your reaction when someone consistently cuts you off midsentence?

[1]Lindenfors, P., Warten, A., and Lind, J. (2021). Dunbar's Number Deconstructed. *Biology Letters* 17(5). https://doi.org/10.1098/rsbl.2021.0158.

- What does eye rolling do to you? That is one area that I have banned in our family—to be a Kubicek means you cannot eye roll, ever.
- How do you handle the negativity of someone close to you?
- How do irrational behavior and exaggerated responses affect you?

Humans have negative and positive attributes occurring almost every day. On the same day you experience negativity, you may experience one of these positive attributes:

- Someone might send you a text telling you how much they love you.
- You could experience someone in your family doing a random act of kindness, like doing the dishes or laundry, when it isn't the norm.
- Someone might send you an unexpected gift to tell you they are thinking of you.
- You may hear someone say something kind about you to someone else, and you didn't know they felt that way.

You get it. People can make you happy or frustrated, often on the same day.

The hope is that those closest to you have not stopped working on self-awareness but continue to work on themselves.

I have found the best way to help others become more self-aware is to be self-aware. One positive person can have a ripple effect on the people around them.

Do you remember those science experiments where the teacher would drop a small rock in a pan of water to explain waves and tsunamis? A cause has effects when one thing makes something else happen. One action causes a reaction, which causes more ripples as the cycle continues.

Susan had had it. She was so frustrated with her husband and his negative mindset. For years she had been covering for him by apologizing to others for his cynical comments and his gruff behavior. Their kids were used to it and began to avoid him while in public. As we met, I asked her all she had done to deal with this negative cycle. She had two responses: 1) she gave him "that look," and 2) she would chide him in the car on the way home.

I asked her how that was working for her after 26 years of marriage, and she got the point. She was constantly apologizing for his actions. The truth was that he didn't have a Purpose, as she was the breadwinner for their family. If she wanted to see a breakthrough, he would have to get healthy—he needed to have a reason to get out of bed in the morning. That was the place to start.

People affect people—either positively or negatively.

When I was 21, I had the chance to usher several world leaders to their seats at the first national prayer breakfast in Moscow after the fall of the Soviet Union. The Dalai Lama was one of those leaders. I like his quote about how to deal with people:

> *"Do not let the behavior of others destroy your inner peace."*
> —*Dalai Lama*

I am often amazed at how strong leaders can allow the negative to continue with the People closest to themselves.

People will make you crazy unless you figure them out.

Unlocking People

I work with a group of professionals worldwide who help people understand how to unlock people so they can increase their trust levels and influence people at home and work.

Because People are complex, they are full of insecurities and drama. Many have underdeveloped personalities or overdeveloped egos. Most are working hard to protect what they have while proving that they belong. In 2011, I wrote a *Wall Street Journal* bestselling book called *Leadership Is Dead* that broke down why people tend to sabotage themselves.[2]

---

[2]Kubicek, J. (2011). *Leadership Is Dead: How Influence Is Reviving It.* New York: Howard Books.

In the book, I explain how most of us are locked up by our self-preservation, which is what we are overprotecting. The premise is that when you overprotect what you are afraid of losing, you will lose it sooner. It is a paradox. Suppose you are fearful of losing your job. In that case, you might overtry, overcommunicate, and, in essence, drive people crazy, which could cause them to easily choose not to employ you at their company any longer.

Self-preservation is insecurity, and it locks people up in the strangest ways. The following three questions can diffuse your self-preservation if you let them:

1. What are you afraid of losing?
2. What are you trying to hide?
3. What are you trying to prove, and to whom?

The truth is that most people in your life are not unlocked, and it is up to you to be a Person of Peace. It can be frustrating to be the adult in the room when you are in a room of "adults." Such is life.

This book aims to help you become the healthiest version of yourself—at Peace deep on the inside. You cannot give what you don't possess. Or, said more positively, we give what we possess.

The key to unlocking others is to be unlocked yourself first. I hope that can happen in these writings. As for your People, well, there is work to be done.

Your Who

Let's get specific to analyze how people affect you, knowing that you and I affect people positively or negatively as well.

To get your People % number, I suggest you hone the list to either your phone Favorites or take your top 10 to 20 people (those you spend the most time with). Create a system like the following example with a ranking of how good you feel about the relationship.

Make a list of your top 10 to 20 people. Without overthinking it, give them a percentage between 1 and 100%:

1. Amanda – 85%
2. Ryan – 80%
3. Mom – 78%
4. Dad – 72%
5. Jarius – 90%
6. Liza – 70%
7. Ramone – 62%
8. Julia – 88%
9. Tate – 95%
10. Allison – 80%

Total all the percentages together and divide by the total number of people on your list to get your People %. From the example:

People Total: 735/10 = 73.5%

This calculation gives you your People number for your overall Peace Index, but it doesn't explain why. Why did you give each person the number you did? You can go as deep as you want to go here. Here are some examples of the quality of the relationship that explains how you got to these numbers.

1. Amanda – 85%. The best place we have been in for a while.
2. Ryan –80%. Solid, but I feel I could be more intentional.
3. Mom – 78%. Good relationship. Not much drama.
4. Dad – 72%. Good; wished we spent more time together.
5. Jarius – 90%. My man. Easy. It feels like we know each other well.
6. Liza – 70%. She is always on her phone and can be petty.

7. Ramone – 62%. So hard. I'm not sure what happened with us.
8. Julia – 88%. She is so fun to be around for all of us.
9. Tate – 95%. SOLID. I wish we had more time.
10. Allison – 80%. Steady eddy. She is consistent.

Be mindful that this is a sensitive list. It can create a lot of drama if you share this list with anyone. It might be best to think about it or burn the paper when completed. Seriously.

The Highest Highs and the Lowest Lows

People are a mess—a beautiful mess. We all are. Remember, you are on someone else's list, and that number might not be that high. That's what makes us so fun and so challenging. We must manage the gold amidst the dirt.

People can bring us to our highest highs and lowest lows, even on the same day. The truth is that People make us who we are. Our parents literally made us and shaped us. Teachers poured ideas and knowledge into us. Friends shape us (for good and bad). Bosses impact us (again, either for good or ill). These people help us develop our skills, shape our personalities, and push us to higher levels than we would have done by ourselves.

Complete the following exercise.

Personal Exercise:

What do your People do to bring you joy?

- uplifting /encouraging
- prayer (intentional)
- positive Outlook

What do your People do that brings you down?

- negative Outlook
- Speak negative
- drain your energy

Turn that around and ask the same questions—what joy do you bring people? Or where do you bring them down?

For, Against, or For Yourself

Communication and trust are the keys to great relationships. Most of us have good intentions but can struggle to show that intent for a myriad of reasons. Your goal for your favorite list should be to convey that you are For Them, not Against Them, or For Yourself.

Establishing being for others develops trust faster, which again leads to Peace on both sides.

I get the privilege of working in sports performance for the University of Oklahoma college football team. During one practice, I watched a coach dress down a player because the player wasn't in the correct position two plays in a row. I went over to the player to check his eyes to see his demeanor. I asked him how he felt to see how the player processed the challenge, and his comment was stunning, "Oh, yeah, I'm good. Coach is for me. He's got my back." He jumped right back in to make a play. That is a healthy relationship.

What about you? Who are those who have been for you, against you, or for themselves?

We relate differently to each of these different motives. And others relate to you differently based on how you make them feel.

Trust is the firm belief in the reliability, truth, ability, or strength of someone or something. If a person doesn't firmly believe that you care for them, they might not trust you the way you hope they would.

Here are some phrases I have heard from people I have counseled through the years that show their emotion toward others who are not for them:

- "My dad never had time for me."
- "She is so insecure and afraid of FOMO [fear of missing out]. It makes her consumed with herself and no one else."

- "He says all the words, but I think he would turn on me in a heartbeat at the end of the day."
- "Everything I say gets nitpicked. I have stopped sharing because I don't want the critique."

On the other end of the spectrum, some positives have been shared with me:

- "Something happened over the past year in my marriage. My wife and I decided to fight for each other, not against each other, and it has changed everything."
- "He is such a good communicator. I know he is busy, but he takes the time to check in to make sure we are aligned. He is a great leader."

A person's intent is so important.

One last story on this subject happened when I was living in London. One new leader I was coaching had a boss who was a bit of a cynic with a formidable reputation, though people liked him over time. The problem was his body language. He had a long face with a big scowl that caused anyone new to put up their walls of self-preservation. I once asked the boss if he was happy, and he said, with a low-key deep voice with no smile, that he was having a fantastic day—it was his birthday. You would have never known.

My point is that people need to know and see that you care for them if you want to be healthy enough to move their People number higher on their peace index.

Relational Dynamics

Between two people are relational dynamics. Those dynamics involve history, status, motivation, relational style, roles, etc. Relationships are so complicated.

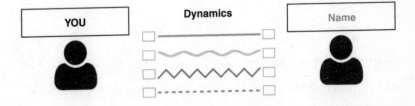

I like to encourage people that any relationship starts with you, not them. As far as you are concerned, it is your job to be at Peace with others. Often that is much harder to say than do.

Steve Cockram and I created a tool to help with these relational dynamics. It is called the Support Challenge Matrix. The idea is that the person who appropriately brings high support with the appropriate high challenge has the best chance for relational success. The other person will respect and appreciate your influence in their life.

© Pub House

High support means that you provide people in your life with what they need to do their job or live their life. That means practical support as well as emotional support. High challenge, on the other hand, is holding people accountable to the agreed upon expectations and motivating them to accomplish those things.

The person who Liberates turns the relationship green—empowerment and opportunity. These people are called "liberating leaders" and they make people better.

The difficulty is that every person is different. Some need more support at times, while others need more challenge. The secret is to learn how to calibrate high support and challenge and situationally adjust to the person.

Sometimes I can Liberate one person, while Dominating another and Protecting another, all in one day. The tool helps you assess and adjust so you can move people toward liberation.

Look at your Favorite People list from earlier in the chapter and ask these questions:

- Where do you think each person would list you on the Support Challenge Matrix?
- Where would you put them and their relational style on the Support Challenge matrix?
- What must happen with each relationship to move it to the top right—Liberate—quadrant?

You must establish high support before you bring high challenges, or the other person will feel you are against them because they experience your challenge first. Your goal in relational dynamics is to learn how to fight for the highest possible good of everyone on the list. Sometimes it is impossible, so you do what you can do to have the best chance to liberate.

Linda was naturally a support person. She over-supported most people in her life, and in return, most people took her for granted. One day she had had enough and moved from high support with no challenge to all challenge with the appearance of no support. Her family started to laugh, and that led to her tears. They had taken her for granted so long that they became entitled. The answer was not in removing support but in learning how to challenge them by sharing her expectations. It took weeks, but she eventually established her voice in her family and began to move her family from protecting to liberating.

Expectations Scale

If you want to improve your People score, you must work on the expectations of each relational dynamic.

Expectations are the anticipation of something you hope happens a certain way. Your expectations can lead to resentment if you haven't communicated them to others effectively.

I like to think of expectations as what you want to happen by whom by when.

We all have them, but most don't share them effectively with others. It is a problem, as it leads to most drama in relational dynamics. Are your expectations realistic, unrealistic, or impossible as you review this tool? Or are they on the other end of the spectrum where you have limited or resigned your relationship expectations?

Resigned	Limited	Realistic	Unrealistic	Impossible

Ask yourself:
What are my expectations on the scale above?
Have I communicated my expectations clearly?

© Pub House

Many of us can have unrealistic expectations about the type of relationship we have with the other party, which leads to a lower People number precisely because someone is not doing something we believe they should be doing. The other person may be completely unaware that they aren't meeting your expectations, which leads to an opportunity to reset by having a clear and concise expectations conversation.

Many men, in general, are unaware of what their high expectations combined with low communication do to the other person. Over time this leads to chemistry gaps as they use more force to get their way, whether at work or home. When the other party doesn't do what they want, they elevate their voice and either dominate or abdicate with the other person, creating misalignment and frustration. Day after day, this pattern continues of doing the same thing, expecting different results.

We must consistently calibrate high support with high challenge to help our People grow.

Go through your top 10 to 20 People list and review it against the Expectations Scale using the same People % numbers from the example in the "Your Who" section earlier in this chapter. Are your expectations Realistic, Unrealistic, or the other—Limited or Resigned?

1. Amanda – 85%. Realistic for both of us.
2. Ryan – 80%. He probably has higher expectations, and he is right.

3. Mom – 78%. Probably a bit unrealistic on my part.
4. Dad – 72%. Limited expectations. He has always been too busy.
5. Jarius – 90%. Realistic.
6. Liza – 70%. Limited expectations are heading to Resigned.
7. Ramone – 62%. Impossible for me. He has probably Resigned.
8. Julia – 88%. Realistic.
9. Tate – 95%. Unrealistic with the recent move.
10. Allison – 80%. Realistic.

When you add a tool to any area, the tool does the heavy lifting. From this exercise comes a potential conversation. The goal is to get Realistic with every person in your world to meet expectations and maintain Peace.

There is a time for everything. Sometimes you need to protect your family because the other person isn't healthy, and boundaries are required, limiting expectations, or resigning due to the other person's behavior.

If you keep the support challenge in mind and learn to calibrate high support and high challenge while sharing your expectations, your chances of relational success will go up immensely.

Responding to Others

Let's go deeper and discuss what happens when someone does something hurtful to you. Say it appears someone is against you. How do you respond?

I love what Jesus of Nazareth says to his guys when they go village to village to help people. By the way, I find that most people miss the incredible work of Jesus because of their prejudgment or fear of religion. He truly is the best example of apprenticeship on record.

He says to his disciples in Matthew 10:12-14, "Greet a household when you enter it, and if the household is worthy, let your Peace be on it; but if it is unworthy, **let your peace return to you.** If anyone does not welcome you or listen to your words, shake the dust off your feet when you leave that house or town."

He was teaching his guy's relational dynamics. Many of us try to make things happen when all we need to do is shake the dust off and move on.

People Plan: You to Others

So how do you help others grow their People number? Landon Lynch, one of our GiANT's in Denver, shares a pertinent story.

An executive client gave himself a 50% on the People score of the Peace Index. He said he didn't want to spend time unpacking it, as it was complicated. The next time we were together, it, hadn't changed, so we rolled up our sleeves and began to work on the issue.

He recognized that he was in a pattern of wanting to have balance and a relationship in his life that gave him support. Still, everything he was communicating and how he was structuring his life was perpetuating a cycle of him getting bored with people when they could no longer be a project. Then he would find other project people for his life and start the process of feeling under-supported all over again.

He decided he would have a difficult conversation with his girlfriend and look at three places in their calendars where he could invest his time more effectively around recharge and focused work. The hope was that there would be less resentment and more presence and intentionality during their time together.

At first, she was a little put off but agreed they were getting into patterns that weren't helping either of them. One month later, the People score jumped from 50% to 80%, and his sense of Purpose and place followed. He realized in one move that People was his driver—his leading indicator. He had been sabotaging his happiness because of the way he was scheduling his life. He said, "This last month has been one of the most unexpected shifts in my whole life. I didn't know I could feel this way. Do you think it could last?"

My client then used the Peace Index to help apprentice his sales leaders during a scheduled review. The guy he was reviewing is younger (mid/late 20s) and has a family. As they worked through it, they discovered that what was low for him was Purpose. As a Pioneer, my client was concerned that his employee was lacking in Purpose because he couldn't imagine staying in a job where he didn't find Purpose. But, come to find out, Purpose was not the Leading Indicator for this guy—People were.

As they talked about the role he was filling, they began to reshape the expectations of his job to allow him some more People time. All of that was great, but I thought the most significant part was that his employee said to him, "You know, this is the longest anyone has ever talked to me about my future." The tool did the heavy lifting and gave them the framework for the breakthrough.

People can affect your Peace Index radically from one day to the next.

So far as it depends on you, be at Peace with all your People.

CHAPTER FOUR

Place: The Spaces That Supercharge Us

Dave and Millicent Gillogly lived half of the year in the Garden of Eden, which just happens to be in Silver Gate, Montana.

Their house was exactly what you picture in a log cabin mountain home. A large fireplace and a large loft for guests. Their backyard was a rolling river, and their front yard was Yellowstone.

I took my son, Will, there when he turned 10 years old. The first day we arrived we saw a bison running through town. On one of our epic fly-fishing trips, we saw signs of grizzly bears everywhere.

Will and I were just visiting for a few days, but the Gillogly's lived there—in paradise.

Every time I saw Dave, he would get the biggest smile on his face because Yellowstone, and his home, filled his cup. It was his happy Place.

One of the most memorable things that Dave would do was to wood burn the names of their guests on a wooden plaque and hang it on the wall going up the stairs. Dave and Millicent shared their Peace often. They allowed others, like Will and me, to experience their space, their Place. And we were grateful. That trip continues to be one of the best experiences of our lives because Dave Gillogly shared his Peace.

Every circle is interconnected. Personal Health can affect Purpose in the same way that People can affect Personal Health, and so forth. Place can radically affect them all. If you don't find Peace in your home, neighborhood, or city, your Peace Index will be lower.

Place keeps us sane, or it's what drives us crazy. We live where we rest unless we can't, creating problems. Place consists of spaces in which you reside.

- Your bedroom.
- Your den or favorite living space.
- Your backyard.
- Your home.
- Your actual office spaces.
- Your favorite restaurant or area of town.

Your Place should be sacred—the space where you can recharge, connect, and be yourself. Your home doesn't have to be grandiose to be amazing; it just needs to fit you.

Before we get into how to make Place special, answer these questions honestly:

- How happy are you with the physical location where you live and work?
- Does it fit you, or is it only for "a season"?
- How peaceful is your house?
- Do you have a place to recharge and think?
- Does your office work for you?

Making Place a Special Place

Place should be recharging, like Dave and Millicent's log cabin. When you walk in and drop your keys and your bags, you should be able to breathe a sigh of relief. You should be able to begin recharging the minute you walk into your home.

My wife and I have tried to turn our homes into respites. One of the areas we have focused on was the backyard. We wanted a safe wonderland for our kids to play in as they were growing up. It was one Place we could control and or enjoy even if the city or location wasn't ideal.

Place is an accumulation of spaces. It is the space needed to nest, rest, eat, gather, and play. Yet it means more than just your room or home; it is also your neighborhood or district. Place reaches into the town, city, and region as well.

I will never forget the reality of moving from Oklahoma City to Atlanta in 2007. The decision to move was a fast one. We moved 40 days after agreeing to move to Atlanta after merging an acquisition into GiANT. We loved our home in Oklahoma and decided on a house in Atlanta because of the following benefits:

- It had a fantastic backyard.
- There was a sideways commute in Atlanta traffic to my office.
- The Chattahoochee River was a quarter mile away.
- The neighborhood has a pool, and the neighbors were friendly.
- We could build out the basement to be a guest area.

My dad always told me that whenever we move, it is crucial to find 1) a good barber, 2) a good banker, and 3) a local family restaurant. We found two out of three. Place includes where you live (your actual house) and the community you enjoy. It is possible to love your house and lament the community or love the community but not enjoy your home. Add to that, your office or work situation quickly makes enjoying Place more complex.

Because Places are spaces, it is essential to be intentional in developing your areas well so that you can truly rest and reset for the work or life you lead.

Hygge

To do that well, I want to introduce a Danish philosophy called Hygge (pronounced Hoo-ga.) The concept revolves around a universal feeling of being warm, safe, comforted, and sheltered that allows us to experience belonging to others and enjoying the moment.

Most have experienced it on a winter night when a loved one made a fire while you cooked a delicious meal and watched the snow. Hygge occurs when your loved one covers you with a blanket while you're taking an afternoon nap. Hygge anchors us, reminding us to slow down and enjoy life. It is a feeling of Peace as you savor the special moment in time with those you care about the most.

When you experience this often, you feel firmly grounded—secure and confident in your surroundings. It creates a bond to your space or Place. These settings make life comfortable and warm.

This connection makes quaint villages great vacation spots that people return to repeatedly. They experience Hygge in a cafe or at a fire pit or walking along the beach. It is rootedness. We thrive in healthy places. Our souls are fed by our friends' smiles and the routines of special breakfast or the smell of our favorite coffee.

The same is true in offices, although harder to create. The office can be sterile and is not as controllable as your home is. You might be given an office or an area to work. The rules have already been established, and the personalities at the office may not value what you value.

However, you can control what you can control.

Lucas Mundt, who works for Simple Modern, famously decided to create a Hygge moment by turning his cubicle into a log cabin look and feel. He had a fake deer head, a mini-fireplace, wood floors, and cabin wallpaper. His intentionality attracted attention from news agencies and social media around the world.

Who says you can't create the type of environment that you have always wanted?

The Importance of Space

To create better spaces, you must be committed and intentional to see it through. Creating spaces takes time, and you must listen to everyone else sharing that space with you to do it well. There is a DIY way to make things work for you.

It starts with addressing these space questions.

- Where do you like to recharge the most in your home?
- What needs to happen to make it feel better to you? Do you need a better chair or a new couch? Does it need to be decluttered?
- What space do you share the most with a significant other, and how can that improve?
- What would make your house a better living space? Do you have a plan for that?
- What would have to happen to take your office space to a higher level of contentment?
- Lastly, what needs to improve in your community to enjoy it more?

As mentioned before, my wife, Kelly, runs a company called Visionary, where she helps people develop spaces. She loves the form and function of how and where you live. She designed our home around how many dinner parties we would have a month and where we needed electrical plug-ins while working either casually or formally. She didn't miss anything. Our home is designed per space to maximize usefulness while being aesthetically pleasing.

Spaces affect us psychologically because most people live accidentally and allow negatives to infringe on their lives. Thus, their Place number is lower, affecting their Peace Index.

I believe our spaces and our Place are the locations where we can let our guards down—where People interact.

If we don't feel secure or safe, we can't recharge effectively. This level of insecurity causes stress where we should feel most comfortable. Therefore, we won't relax well and reset for the next day and, ultimately, we'll feel depleted day after day.

Reviewing Your Place and Space

How would you rank each space in your Place from 1 to 100% (100% being the highest)?

- Your bedroom.
- Your den or favorite living space.
- Your backyard.

- Your house.
- Your actual office spaces.
- Your favorite restaurant or area of town.

Here are my accumulated scores as of today and the explanation as to why:

- Your bedroom – 80%. We are still finishing the final details.
- Your den or favorite living space – 90%. I have multiple spots.
- Your backyard – 95%. It is perfect when the weather is nice.
- Your house – 95%. It fits us perfectly.
- Your actual office space – 80%. It is an incredible film studio, but it may be too hipster for me. I want a conference room.

Your favorite restaurant or area of town – 65%. This is the lowest area as we don't have "our" restaurant or spot yet.

Average Place % Number: 505/6 = 84%

I suggest you create your Place number here:

- Your bedroom: _____
- Your den or favorite living space: _____
- Your backyard: _____
- Your house: _____
- Your actual office spaces: _____
- Your favorite restaurant or area of town: _____
- Place % Number (add the numbers together and divide by six): _____

Robert lives an hour away from his office. He is an executive who has had a two-hour commute each day for over 25 years. He and his wife are empty nesters, and while they enjoy their spaces in their home, they are a bit tired of their home, disconnected from their neighborhood, and have very little community in their town of 30,000 people.

They have very little reason to stay in the town where their house is. They are excited about the possibility of moving to the city, which brings more restaurants and fun for their stage of life. After reviewing their Place number on the Peace Index, they are fully committed to moving.

What about you?

Control the Controllable

Controlling what you can control applies to every circle. Control what you can control within your Purpose, People, Personal Health, and Provision. This concept is especially pertinent to Place. Listen to Sophie Preston, a Brit living in the United States, share her story of controlling what she could control with her space.

It was March 2020, just before the chaos, and I felt off. I had been traveling to England with my then 2-year-old son, Isaiah. We returned to Oklahoma to quarantine, which then turned into living inside the 1495-square-foot house with my husband and son for 17 weeks. There was nothing wrong with the house other than its size. We walked and played outside every day, but the inside was a mess per my standards. We were in a cramped situation with John's military ventures, football memorabilia, and both being first-time parents. Like much of the world, we did our best to work and parent from home. John was working on his lap in the mancave, I was working from the dining room table or the kitchen counter, and Isaiah was living his best life all over the house. I didn't mention we have a 23-pound "Ragdoll" cat named King roaming. Regardless of their leading peace indicator, I think anyone would agree (and maybe resonate) that this was a rough situation.

I was in the middle of implementing GiANT's tools within a state government agency and hosting numerous one-hour sessions on the Peace Index to assist with the general "robbing" of Peace we all felt that year. Like many facilitators, I plan to live the tools first and tell my stories of their validity. I sat down among the toddler activities, books, and clothes and worked around the Peace Index with a cat on my lap. Putting a number to the indictors made it real, and I was able to identify my current sense of Place was at a 50. I still felt lucky to have a job, health, and a healthy family as many were experiencing loss. But this was a tool for me at that moment, and I couldn't lie to myself about how I felt about my surroundings.

For me, Place needs to be "just so" or else I can feel on edge, uncomfortable, unable to rest, and even flighty (literally—I had just flown back to England with almost no notice because, I now know, my send of Place was low). The Place robbed me of my overall Peace Index daily and affected so many other areas of my life. I took this to John and said, "LOOK! THIS IS IT!" and he agreed in his Guardian/Creative mind that acting was the logical thing to do: we had outgrown the space, we were only going to grow as a family, and who knew how long we would be working from home.

We immediately placed our house on the market. Within months, we were packed up and ready to move into double the space. I am grateful to the Peace Index for these reasons:

1. *I learned that I'm constantly feeling a "Place deficit" as an immigrant. I can now identify some of my behaviors, like spontaneously leaving for England for weeks out of the year, as me seeking higher Peace in Place. I can use this tool to see it coming and become more intentional.*

2. *Serving the Place indicator also served Provision; we acted at the perfect time, scoring a great mortgage deal and house price that financially benefits our future.*

3. *The Peace Index is the first step in having hope; like me, I've witnessed many who felt "off," stuck, and hopeless identify their leading indicator robbing their overall Peace and creating the pathway to Peace.*

Some say: "I could never quite tell what was getting me down." It's personal; you are in control. It's specific, whittled down to one area. It's immediate; how you are at this moment.

It is so rewarding to hear people like Sophie share their stories of a breakthrough with a simple but powerful concept. When you get honest with yourself, you can make significant progress in your life.

Dealing with the Uncontrollable

What happens when things are uncontrollable? How do you deal with tornadoes, hurricanes, earthquakes, floods, or fires? I have known someone personally affected by each of these.

Add mold issues or toxic neighbors, and suddenly, your Place is under attack.

What happens when People who impact your Place move away? Your favorite neighbors can impact you significantly. One of our guides, Ryan Mayfield, shares the story of how this affected his family:

> My best friend and his family (our family's best friends collectively) moved from Arkansas to Wisconsin last September. Up until that point, we were very content in our Place. As soon as they left, our Place score was impacted and became the leading indicator of our Peace Index. We didn't realize how much they were anchoring us where we were. When they left, we weren't as tied to our community anymore. This all translated into a time of noticeably lower scores, which showed themselves in real life. We decided to pull the trigger on making a move to Tulsa—something we had dreamed about before but never seriously considered. We realized that was the right move for our family, so we are in the process of moving now. Our friends kept our Place high. Without them, it was time to move.

Can anyone else relate to that?

Here is my point. Many of you stay in situations that aren't healthy. You can change, but you may not think you can. I believe in our current era that most people should review their life and make changes to improve the areas that they can. So, let's dream.

Dream Space Exercise

Let's make this conversation real. If your Place circle is low on your Peace Index, I want you to list what is explicitly lower. What area(s) needs to improve? Think through the majors and the minors and create a game plan to enhance your Place as quickly as possible.

- Your bedroom.
- Your den or favorite living space.
- Your backyard.
- Your house.
- Your actual office spaces.
- Your favorite restaurant or area of town.

Once you have done this, ask those closest to you to do the same process. Ask the other person, or people, to do that independently of you so that you can be objective and see the areas that they believe need to improve. The process might be life-altering. Together you may realize that you have been settling for second best when you had the opportunity to improve your life.

Now, let's work to increase your Peace in Personal Health.

CHAPTER FIVE

Personal Health: Choosing Something Better

Recently I received some shocking news. An executive I interviewed recently at a global industry conference died, suddenly, of a heart attack.

I couldn't believe it. I was just with him, and I had thought we were the same age (and I am young!)

It is surreal because of all the other presenters, he and I hit it off especially. We grabbed a coffee and talked about family, our workout regimen amidst the travel, and the world at large.

Weeks later, he had died.

Peace is fragile when it comes to our Personal Health, especially when you have just experienced death. This one affected me. Not because of a friendship, but rather because we were the same age and he looked to be in great shape.

Our Personal Health is complicated. It combines more than the outer suit of our body; it also is impacted by our mind and spirit. Our natural wiring (personality) mixed with our upbringing and experiences show how we feel about our Personal Health.

In this instance of sudden death, there was more going on than what I could see. As for you, what words would describe your health right now?

Here are some answers I have received from others:

"I don't honestly think about it. I'm just focused on my work."

"I would say good in some areas and bad in others."

"Well, I wasn't dealt a good hand with my genetics and am fighting things that others don't have to fight."

"I feel great. I am finally focused on my health."

"I could lose some pounds right now."

After this one-question survey, I asked each person what Personal Health encompassed to them. Each of them said "physical health" (body). They didn't consider Mental Health (mind) or Spiritual Health (spirit), which I believe most people will say when they think of the word "health."

Personal Health tends to be the lowest number on the Peace Index because most people think about their physical health when they get to this circle. Advertising shows that health is an issue as commercials litter television with drug ads claiming to help with diabetes, heart attacks, anxiety, fat loss, etc.

One Thing Affects Another

The fact is that our Personal Health is more than physical alone. We are made of mind, body, and spirit. Each of these is interconnected where one affects the others.

Have you ever opened the hood on your vehicle, amazed at all the wires, hoses, and parts linked to a complex technology? That is us. We are connected by our physical to our mental and emotional to our spiritual. All play a role in our overall health. If you focus on one area while ignoring another, you most likely won't resolve the issue.

Ryan was consumed with working out. He focused on his body relentlessly. After coaching him for a while, I asked him about this extreme focus. He exclaimed it was a release valve from the pressure of his job. The more stressed, the more he worked out in the gym. Over time I began to see that the physical overfocus was due to an underfocus on his emotional and spiritual health.

Without giving too much detail, Ryan had a rough upbringing and was proving to everybody that he could start a business and "pull himself up by his bootstraps." He had some deep hatred and unforgiveness that caused him to be hard to work for, which caused employees stress because of his behavior, which in turn had Ryan taking more time out of the office to work out to alleviate his stress. All of this led to more disconnection because of his absence, which caused havoc when Ryan would return to work with things not happening as he had hoped. That just caused his workout refresh time to be wiped away. It was a vicious cycle.

Six months later, things had begun to improve. It was simple and complicated at the same time. Ryan committed to working on his self-awareness through our GiANT tools. I began to show him he was not sharing expectations with his team but blowing up like a volcano when they didn't do what he didn't share but hoped they would do.

We made some adjustments, elevated one team member, and then started to work on the deeper areas of resentment. The hatred was killing him. Over some time, things improved dramatically. We began to work on the spiritual, which led to many breakthroughs and impacted his mental and emotional health. People began to trust him and even like him, and over some time, he began to enjoy himself as well.

It took about 14 months to see the breakthrough occur. Ryan worked out less, which was a good thing in this case. He balanced out his mindset with his heart and his body. Not only did Ryan benefit, but everyone else in his life got to enjoy him.

Personal Health is interrelated. One affects the other. If you ignore one, it will have an effect. Add to that global chaos and ask yourself how each of these has impacted your Personal Health:

- Covid: How did (or does) the pandemic affect you in each of the following areas?
  - Mental Health: _____
  - Physical Health: _____
  - Spiritual Health: _____
- Lockdowns: What was the impact?
  - Mental Health: _____
  - Physical Health: _____
  - Spiritual Health: _____
- Financial Stress: If applicable, how does it affect each area?
  - Mental Health: _____
  - Physical Health: _____
  - Spiritual Health: _____

Asset or Liability

Our health can help us (be an asset) or hurt us (be a liability). We can work to make it more of an asset or ignore it, and it will become more of a liability. It is our choice.

To make our health an excellent or valuable part of our life takes work, and I think that is why most people don't do it. I often use the illustration of raising a puppy. If you don't invest the time and energy to train your dog, you will have a rough 7 to 10 or more years. Ignore dog training discipline at your peril as you lose shoes, sleep, and friends.

On the other hand, if you will do the hard work in the first months and years, you will be so grateful for the rest of your life. The more you put in (in most cases), the more you get out.

The same is true with your health. Our health can be an asset, an advantage for the rest of our life, or not. The key is your mindset. It is a mind shift as most of us have grown up with some prejudice toward one of the categories discussed in the following sections. Maybe it was a parent who scoffed at mental/emotional health. You might have grown up in an unhealthy family where bags of chips were an entree. Or, quite possibly, you had some drama related to spiritual health because of a bad experience or some wound that happened from someone in your family.

However, what if there was something you were missing because of some old grudge or experience? If you shift your mindset, you open to a higher Personal Health score that could affect your entire Peace Index.

Mental Health Mindset

Mental health has been a stigma for some time. The stereotype of a mental hospital with an unstable person in a straitjacket didn't help this issue. The truth is that mental health issues are common.

According to the National Institute of Mental Health, nearly one in five U.S. adults live with a mental illness (52.9 million in 2020).[1] Mental illnesses include many different conditions that vary in severity, ranging from mild to moderate to severe, from depression to bipolar disorder to schizophrenia.

Mild and moderate forms of mental health are being discussed more openly than ever before. It probably helps when stars like Katy Perry, Justin Bieber, or Dwayne "The Rock" Johnson share their anxiety issues that have led to depression. That makes the subject less taboo while giving people hope that they can overcome.

These issues are exacerbated in a pandemic or crisis, as disruption leads to cycles of unrest. Mental health is a topic that needs to be talked about openly to help people heal.

A recent poll of 2,000 men conducted by OnePoll and the accompanying article by Study Finds found that the

---

[1]National Institute of Mental Health. Office of Science Policy, Planning, and Communications, Bethesda, MD. www.nimh.nih.gov.2.

average man rates his mental health at 60% and feels down at least three times per week.[2] The study shares that 57% of men would like to see more support for mental health struggles. In the article, these men claim that consistent conversations with family and friends and lowering their alcohol consumption would help them become more mentally fit.

My goal is to help you train your mind to have more Peace—to live a healthier life with your Purpose, People, Place, Personal Health, and Provision.

> *The more external unrest, the more internal unrest*

The more external turmoil around you, the more unrest in you. Worry, anxiety, and catastrophizing of the future are issues that a nonstable mental mindset can provoke.

I am currently working with a person to help them eradicate negativity from his life. It is a journey indeed. He had a great childhood, but his personality makes him fret details. If he gets overloaded, his view of the future can get cloudy, and he can become short with others. To change his mindset, I asked him to list the areas he is nervous about and the

[2]Study Finds. (2022). Not OK: Average man rates his mental health just 6 out of 10, feels down 3 times a week. (29 April). https://www.studyfinds.org/men-mental-health-feels-down/ (accessed 29 April 2022).

percent likelihood of it occurring. After reviewing the list with him, he smiled as overall his realized his three negative issues had only a 33% chance of happening.

We brought the issues into the light in a safe place and dealt with them one by one. I have been training this person to deal with a negative issue straight on and not allow himself to trust his irrational tendency. He is working on his mind so he can deal with future issues. I hope he begins to see his tendencies and understand the patterns that cause him to be negative and when it occurs so that he can work to alter his actions. That will change the consequences and shape a better reality for him.

Chapter 8, Keeping the Peace, presents a daily system you can use to help you build a healthy mindset to bring consistent Peace to your life.

Physical Health Mindset

Working with athletes has changed the way I communicate with leaders in general. Committed athletes operate differently from other people. They understand that their bodies are assets, and those I have worked with ensure that they develop themselves to the highest level possible.

My son, Will, recently graduated as a business major and decathlete from the University of Oklahoma. A decathlete must perfect 10 events (pole vault, 110-meter hurdles, javelin, high jump, long jump, 400-meter run, 100-meter dash, discus, shot put, and the dreaded 1500-meter run).

Will and his teammates are committed. They eat better than anyone I know; they work out daily, consistently, and help each other get better. It is a different mindset.

I am not suggesting we try to become decathletes, though I think it would be hilarious to create a reality show with everyday people trying 10 track events.

Rather, I suggest an intentional mindset—a healthy view of what we eat and drink and how we rest. We can work to think like an athlete while living our everyday lives.

This mindset, for me, has been a shift into preplanning. I think about my exercise plans the night before. I think about what I will eat and won't eat. Even though I am not running a race, I desire to have the healthiest body possible for the longest time.

There are so many good physical health books and systems available. *The Naked Code* by Bronson Taylor is a short, powerful example of the resources available. I am just trying to motivate you to strengthen one-third of your Personal Health number through a little intentional living.

Spiritual Health Mindset

Health is a person's overall condition. When we say Personal Health, we mean the holistic state of a person (mental, physical, spiritual, emotional health). What if you only focus on one out of three? What if you were a physical beast but mentally unstable and spiritually aloof? That isn't a well-rounded person. Or imagine you are mentally and spiritually astute but out of shape with some problematic real health issues. Your influence is limited in this case.

Even as Jesus matured, he grew in both body and spirit, in favor with God and man, which means that he grew mentally, physically, spiritually, and socially (Luke 2:52).

The spiritual component is fundamental—mind, body, and *spirit*. The spirit is the nonphysical part of a person, the seat of emotions and character, the soul. Many people struggle with anxiety or depression because of physical or soul issues. The soul issues are spiritual. When a person is unsettled in their spirit, it comes from unanswered questions, disappointments, or a crisis of belief.

Years ago, I coached a young professional with a fantastic role inside a large global business. She was a workout machine—probably a bit too much. She is a bright and articulate professional who has gained her peers' respect and influence. The only issue was that she had a hole in her heart—not a literal hole, but a spiritual one. Something was missing. And in her unsettling, she sought some counsel as she processed.

She had grown up with spiritual beliefs but had not made them hers, and she was seeking. The issue was that they were her parents' beliefs, and she realized she had not done the work to develop her own beliefs. Eventually, she settled the issues and was no longer divided. Coincidentally, she began to exercise less while focusing on her emotions and spirit.

The spiritual is vital. It is soul development. This type of development comes in a community, in critical input and daily reflection. Again, Chapter 8 can help with this process when you are ready.

What needs to change in you as it relates to your spiritual development? Do you need to remove the worry from the center of your heart? Do you need friends to help you grow here? Spiritual growth can raise the Peace Index score to higher levels dramatically.

You Affect Your Health Outcome

> *Your Personal Health is either a competitive advantage or daily liability.*

Your Personal Health is either a competitive advantage or daily liability. It is your choice.

Your Personal Health puts you in a position to thrive, or it limits your abilities to flourish. Some may have been born with certain physical or mental limitations. They can teach us how to overcome adversity and maintain mental health more than I ever could. Many are amazing in using limitations as inspiration to grow.

However, for those not born with certain physical or mental limitations, let me ask you this: What are you doing in your life that limits your competitive advantage or creates a health liability? Why is that occurring?

You control the levels of the intentionality of how you treat your body, mind, and spirit. Remember, accidental living is easy initially and miserable in the end.

Trade Up

If you would like some life hacks on getting healthier, consider the idea of Trading Up. I first wrote about Trading Up in *5 Gears*, co-written with Steve Cockram. The idea is that everything we do has a natural Trade Up. Choose an apple instead of a candy bar; a podcast over negative news; a walk over the couch, etc. Incremental changes can add up over time to make a big difference. Consistency is the key.

Personal Health is about choosing the right inputs that help you grow physically, mentally, and spiritually so that your outputs are helpful. Wrong inputs tend to create poor outcomes.

A saying I have always taught our kids reiterates this point. The constant mantra is "Good friends. Good Decisions. Good Life. Bad Friends. Bad Decisions. Bad Life." They often see GF. GD. GL. as a reminder of this idea. We all know it is true. The input of friends creates an output of good decisions.

Trade Up to better decisions and notice that your Peace will improve as well.

Your Personal Health Number

Let's review the Personal Health Number now that you have the information provided in this chapter. Give yourself a number from 1 to 100% (100% as the highest) as it relates to each of these in you:

- Mental Health: _____
- Physical Health: _____
- Spiritual Health: _____

Now, add all three numbers up and divide by three to get your Personal Health Number.

- Total:

Here is where I am today while writing this chapter and why:

- Mental Health: 85%. Chapter 8 will explain why
- Physical Health: 82%. I am being consistent in working out
- Spiritual Health: 90%. Feeling connecting to God in my spirit
- Total: 257/3 = 85.6% Personal Health

Find the Friend

Who is the person you will talk through this with who you trust deeply? Give them their own copy of the book so they can review it with you. Personal Health needs accountability partners—people who will bring high support and high challenge.

Humans tend to drift back to the most comfortable levels possible. Do the hard work of being intentional and find the friend who can help you maximize the asset that is your Personal Health.

Your Personal Health Plan

What do you need to do in each category below? What is the one takeaway from this chapter that is motivating and you can start tomorrow?

- Mental Health: _____
- Physical Health: _____
- Spiritual Health: _____

How can you live life to the fullest with nothing to fear?

CHAPTER SIX

Provision: Nothing to Fear

When it comes to Provision (having what you need), there are three types of People:

1. Those who have more than enough resources. They have so much that they are not aware how much money they fritter away because they don't think about it because they don't need to think about it.

2. Those who have what they need but would like a little (or a lot) more. These are the people who can make ends meet but they think about those needs regularly with the occasional fear that they might not have enough. They usually do.

3. Those who live paycheck to paycheck and go without, without telling others. These are the people who have grown accustomed to sacrificing to help their kids or family, hoping for days when they don't have to think about the basics of food or transportation or a place to live.

When I lived in Moscow, Russia, as a 21-year-old, I lived off $700 per month. I didn't have excess, but I had what I needed. I also wanted to have more provisions. That is when I met Fatorma Siafa.

Fatorma was a refugee from Liberia. The Soviet Union would sponsor Africans to study there, and he was now stuck in Moscow with thousands of other Africans. When the Soviet empire dissolved, so did the scholarship money.

I first met Fatorma in our small International Fellowship church that was held each week in a movie theater. Over time, Fatorma would become the steward of the benevolence work to others who didn't have Provisions. We would give monies and Fatorma would dole it out appropriately as we worked to help these stranded students make it back to their home countries.

Each Sunday we would ask Fatorma if he had what he needed and each week he would smile and say, "I have what I need. I just want to help others get what they need to survive." One of our friends didn't make it. Malnutrition set in and we were too late to help. As an American, I couldn't fathom what I was experiencing each week— people not having what they need to simply live.

Do you have enough?

Do you need more?

Interesting questions. You might ask, "Enough what?" That is what Provision means—having enough of what you need to do what you do.

The amazing ending to the story of Fatorma is that he now lives in Pennsylvania, working as a Chick-fil-A operator. Years ago, I went to visit him and guess what? I met person after person who told me Fatorma had helped them get what they needed.

Because of one man they received what they needed.

How about you? Do you have what you need?

- Did you start a job in a new city, realizing that the costs of a growing family could outstrip the initial excitement of your salary?
- Do you have a cost that was not on the radar that hit you like a rogue wave, knocking you off balance?
- Was there an accident that insurance won't cover?

Most of us experience some sort of surprise in our life, whether when we were younger or because of some dependents in our lives. Kids cost money, and money doesn't grow on trees, to the dismay of our kids.

Your Provision % may simply be getting lower and lower based on the season of life you are living, and that alone could be lowering your Provision score.

In the context of the Peace Index, Provision is your satisfaction level with what you are earning (your income) and what means you have available to live your life, lead your family (if applicable), and do your work.

**PROVISION
%**

Provision is your satisfaction level with what you are earning (your income) and what means you have available to live your life, lead your family (if applicable), and do your work.

So, what is your number? Be honest. Are you at 85% (feeling good) or 70% (just okay), or below 50% (really struggling)?

Let's work on this number, as thinking about Provision can lead to significant breakthroughs. I ultimately want you to be free from any wrong thinking plaguing you around money or finances.

Needs Versus Wants

Let's get started: How much do you need to earn?

When I ask this question to people exploring how to become certified in GiANT as a coach or consultant, they usually say, "$10,000 per month." I then ask them if that is what they want or what they truly need. Inevitably it leads to, "Well, that would be helpful." They then state that they want more. Now, I get it. I have said the same things many times, but the facts are that most of us don't know what we truly need to live on. Life and bills and expenses add up as we pile on new entertainment subscriptions and pay for those unexpected expenses.

It is much easier to list what we want instead of understanding what we need. My wife and I are empty nesters and only have a couple of more payments on college before we are free from the burden of those meddling expenses. We have decided to revisit our budget to truly understand what Provisions we need to do what we do. I could live in a 1000-square-foot home with a guitar, stacks of books, and my computer. Oh, and a fire pit. That is all I truly need.

We have needs, and those are real. But the wants tend to take over the needs because if you are a family, you have three to five or more sets of needs and wants, all clouding the bigger question of "How much do you truly need?"

Where Pressure Resides

Longing for more is what global marketing budgets are designed to provoke. There is pressure to want. Our eyes are attracted to the glimmer and shimmer of clever ads promoting most things we don't need.

For some, longing for more is an addiction. It is like a consumption habit. You don't know why you spend money on things you barely want but don't need. It just happens.

For some, longing for more is a fear of not having enough. Like a squirrel preparing for winter, you want to ensure you have enough Provision to last through a downturn, which isn't unwise.

> *Most of us live under the pressure of not having what we want while just having enough of what we need.*

For some, longing for the basics is a daily prayer. You literally don't have enough to make ends meet and wants are a Christmas list or a dream.

Most of us live under the pressure of not having what we want while just having enough of what we need. And that creates the pressure—the stress that can affect our behavior or cause a smile to a frown.

My struggles with Provision have consumed me my entire life. I grew up in a middle-class family in a smaller town (Shawnee) outside of a smaller city (Oklahoma City). I had everything I needed, and as an only child, I tended to get most of what I wanted. My parents owned small businesses and real estate, and a farm. My dad also worked in the city for the state government. Again, I had everything I needed.

The intriguing part was that I had friends who had much more than I did. Even though I had more than enough for one, they had things I didn't. In college, my family made some career choices that affected my view of what we had versus what we needed. I was going to a more expensive private college, and the pressure to help my family was just on me, not from my parents but my fears. "Did I have enough?"

The fear of not having enough has been a pressure that has not added one helpful thing to my life. I have had everything I have needed and most of what I have wanted, yet I want more. Why is that the case?

Does anyone else deal with this?

Contentment

Say this out loud if it is true. "I have everything I need." "I have enough Provisions to do what I need to do."

To be satisfied and at Peace with your:

- Life
- Marriage
- Career
- Children
- Friendships

- Future
- Possessions, etc.

Mick Jagger quipped the famous lyrics,

"I can't get no satisfaction / Cause I try, and I try, and I try, and I try / I can't get no, I can't get no, satisfaction"

What if you could find contentment?

To be content means to be in a state of happiness and satisfaction. Content with what you have because it is what you need and fits what you want.

So, let me ask you again: Are you satisfied with your current income level and the state of your finances? Are your needs being met?

I recognize this chapter might be uncomfortable, especially if worry for money has become lodged in your heart.

Surviving to Thriving

According to World Vision, there are 689 million people worldwide currently living in extreme poverty, surviving on less than $1.90 a day. That is astounding in the twenty-first century.[1]

---

[1]Peer, A. (2021). Global poverty: Facts, FAQs, and how to help. World Vision (updated 23 August 21). https://www.worldvision.org/sponsorship-news-stories/global-poverty-facts#facts (accessed 2 May 2022).

Abraham Maslow was an American psychologist who developed a hierarchy of needs to explain human motivation. His hierarchy is used globally as foundational research to help people in multiple situations. Here is the premise he taught.[2]

All of us have needs. They start with the physiological needs of food, water, warmth, and rest. The next set includes the needs of security and safety. These are basic, foundational needs that aren't found in many third-world countries, areas of extreme drought, or war-torn lands. In most first-world countries, these are assumed at birth.

The feeling that we don't have what we need can get muddied in our heads so quickly. It can be easy to ignore real needs we have by shaming ourselves for wanting them since we have so much compared to so many in the world. Often, it can be helpful to break down needs through the lens of Maslow's hierarchy to allow ourselves to get really clear about what it is that we feel is lacking. Sometimes the result is healthy perspective and greater contentment with what we have; other times the process helps identify where our dissatisfaction lies so we can do something about it.

---

[2]Cherry, K. (2022). Maslow's Hierarchy of Needs. Verywell Mind (updated 14 February). https://www.verywellmind.com/what-is-maslows-hierarchy-of-needs-4136760 (accessed 2 May 2022).

Do you have enough Provision at this point? Do you have food, water, warmth, and rest? Are you safe and secure?

If not, then your Provision score could be deficient, or it is all you know, and you have learned how to thrive and survive amidst inadequate Provision. If so, Provision most likely becomes the number one priority until you have enough to take care of your responsibilities.

Maslow discussed the next set of needs as psychological. They revolve around belonging, love, and esteem, including intimate relationships and friends, prestige, and a feeling of accomplishment.

You may have had your base needs met, but not your psychological needs. This lack of intimacy could affect how you deal with people and create trust issues in certain situations. It may also affect your views of contentment regarding having what you need.

To thrive means that your self-actualization needs are or have been met. Those needs include achieving your potential in life. That means you know your Purpose and can attain creative activities that make life fulfilling.

It is hard to imagine for many of us living in first-world countries or regions that most of the world will not have the opportunity to achieve our self-actualization needs. Most people can't control their destinies due to poverty, national dictums, family pressures, etc.

Having Enough to Do What You Do

Those with a clear vision of what they want tend to work backward to ensure they have the Provisions needed to accomplish what they want to do. The wise person doesn't get sucked into the lifeless rat race of accumulation and become content with who they are and what they desire. This lot is indeed a small number of people.

Understanding what you need versus what you want is an act of adulting, even if you are an older adult. I have been training my three 20-somethings about prioritizing what is essential and what is not for years. They are now getting to experience it. Unfortunately, most adults never adult, which is why there is so much debt, waste, and unfruitful living. Peace rarely exists when adults are not living as adults.

Knowing What You Want

What else do you want? There are generic wishes like wanting a new iPhone or a new car. Those wants are different than the philosophical wants—what you want for your life. What you want for your life might be to have a happy family or for your marriage to be more vital. You might want to unlock your full potential in your career while also wanting a bigger house.

What you want for your life leads to vision. The wants of life are called possessions, and there is a big difference. Once you figure out your vision (what you want for your life), you can work to become more responsible with money to obtain your wants. You can proactively work backward by listing your provisions and being a steward of what you need.

That is why budgeting is helpful for many. You can see what you have and what you need and prioritize what you want. It takes real vision—the imagination of what doesn't exist but that which you want to happen.

The goal is to understand what you need and be content with what you have.

Most people never have enough. They are not disciplined to not waste money on petty items that don't help them get where they want to go because these individuals don't know where they want to go.

Getting on the Same Page

People have different perspectives on money, saving, investments, etc., which makes Provision a complex topic to discuss. Getting on the same page is essential with those closest to you. That is why you must do the hard work to communicate, build relational trust, and work toward alignment that meets your vision and financial goals.

Here are the issues that tend to make it challenging to align with others in your life.

- Your spouse spends frivolously but gets defensive and feels attacked by you when you try to have the conversation.
- You and your spouse are not good with money and become diligent in some seasons and carefree in others, which brings money woes and creates chaos.
- Each person has a different view of priorities. The hot tub in the backyard might be high on one list, while a new bedroom set is more critical in the other person's mind.
- One person might be calling a Want a Need, which leads to lower Peace levels because of conflicts in how to spend money.

Provisions, when stewarded well, bring long-term wealth. Wealth brings options. Options are choices. Working together with those you love intentionally and responsibly brings Peace in droves. It allows your Peace Index to rise because your Provision % increases. If you and those closest to you are aligned and move forward confidently because you know what you want and understand your needs, you will maximize your Provision.

Now, retake the Provision assessment (give each statement a number from 1 to 100%).

- How good do you feel about what you are currently earning from your work: *100*

- You have the resources needed to do what you desire to do in life: *95*

- How hopeful are you about your future provisions in light of your current reality: *95*

Add all three numbers and divide by three to get an up-to-date Provision score.

What is your Provision % now? *98*

Did it increase from the assessment in the first chapter?

Be Careful of the Purpose and Provision Clash

Be careful that your Purpose and Provision don't take you down a road of hopelessness. I can give you over 100 examples where I have met with someone who doesn't know what they want to do in their life and are in a "dead-end job," making a low salary, which leads to hopeless chaos.

To help them is like unwinding a tangled ball of yarn. Because they need the money (often because of poor financial decisions like excessive car payments or overspending on a home), they stay in the job and complain rather than do the hard work of dusting off their vision.

When a person reaches this level, they can get trapped in the doom loop where they don't know their Purpose and feel the weight of needed Provision. Chaos must be conquered so Peace can enter. If this is you, then here are two things I recommend:

1. Meet twice a month with the wisest person you know, either paid or unpaid.
2. Have them help you see the doom loop and work with them to find the root cause of any current issue.

Break the list down to the real dissatisfactions/issues and begin answering these questions:

1. What is the real problem here?
2. How did you get there? (Without blame or judgment)
3. What are two or three possible solutions to solve it?
4. Who else needs to help solve this?
5. When will you resolve it?

Have your friend/counselor begin to help you work on your Purpose. Revisit Chapter 2, Purpose, and work through these questions:

1. What are you made to do?
2. What current opportunities are available that you could pursue that connect more to your passions and expertise?
3. Are there any mindset changes you can make that could positively affect how you view your current job?

Provision is about security. When you are insecure, it is hard to see the world correctly. When working with sports teams, I use the concept of Scurry vs. Hustle. When a team is scurrying, they worry, and they tend to mess up when they worry. Conversely, when a team is hustling, they are focused and confident. They are in the zone.

Are you scurrying? Do the hard work of conquering the chaos related to your insecurity and low confidence. That will allow you to focus on your strengths and begin to hustle.

Now, let's move to Your Peace Plan. The next chapter is designed to help you put all of your learning together to conquer chaos and increase your Peace.

CHAPTER SEVEN

Your Peace Plan

Every sports team has an offensive and defensive strategy they use to win. The offense gives the team options to score more points. The defense creates strategies to keep the other team from scoring.

As we work on your Peace Plan, we need to think about both offense and defense. Offense means you are intentionally working on initiatives to increase your Peace levels. Defense for you personally means creating the boundaries and systems you need to protect you, your spouse, or your family from any drama or negativity.

The final Peace Plan at the end of this chapter will help you tremendously by creating an action plan with a minimum of two or three significant changes to create higher levels of Peace and one or two minor areas for Purpose, People, Place, Personal Health, or Provision.

Getting to Your Number

At the beginning of the book, you calculated your Peace Index by giving yourself a 1 to 100% (100% being the highest) for how well you felt about each category (Purpose, People, Place, Personal Health, and Provision). You then added them up and divided them by five to reveal your Peace Index number.

After going through each chapter and working on some ways to improve, I want you to retake the test. Go back through the Peace Index in this graphic, give yourself a % number (1 to 100%, with 100% being the highest) for each category. Aggregate all the numbers and divide by five to get your updated Peace Index number.

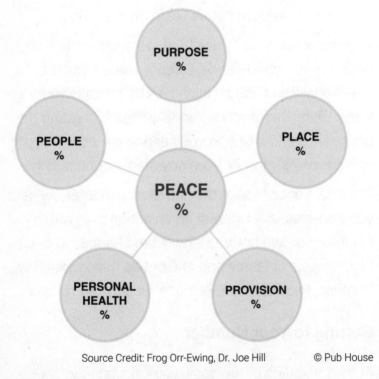

Source Credit: Frog Orr-Ewing, Dr. Joe Hill   © Pub House

Did your Peace Index change? Did it go up or down?

Your Driver

All categories in the Peace Index are not equal. Some are more important to you than others. One of them tends to be the key driver for you, which means that category affects everything in your life. If it is off, then every number could be affected by it negatively, and conversely, if it is positive.

Which of the five categories in the Peace Index is your driver—the most essential segment that affects you more than the others?

Purpose and People tend to be drivers for most people when I survey them during my presentations.

Purpose is my driver. If my Purpose % is high, I can put up with less than exciting things. My energy tends to be high, and I am considerably easier to live with (says my wife). However, if my Purpose is off, everything will be off.

Our last year in Atlanta was excruciating. I had lost my Purpose, and I could feel it. Almost eight years earlier, my Purpose was at an all-time high. We had just bought John Maxwell's businesses, and there I was building the Leadercast brand and growing the Catalyst conferences. We had a group of highly motivated People doing exceptional work as we were completing a turnaround. The Place was great, as we were close to mountains and the beach and we really enjoyed our house, especially the backyard. Personal Health was fine, and Provision was good even though our costs were higher in Atlanta.

All in all, my Purpose was at 92% my first year in Atlanta. Seven-and-a half years later, I was at 60%. Every year I began to lose more and more of my Purpose. I had let the business define me. Any loss was personal, and my stress crept up higher and higher even as we had success after success. I lost my Purpose as I became a manager rather than a creative visionary.

When my Purpose began to slide, my Peace Index dropped. I began to notice and complained about the traffic even more. It was more humid suddenly. Again, I didn't see it when my Purpose was high. The People were all fantastic but tied to the work I was starting to despise. I was losing my Purpose. My Personal Health was sliding measurably into a stress land mine. Even though the Provision was acceptable, it didn't matter as everything else was moving down.

What did I do about it? I fired myself. Truly.

I communicated to my board that it was time to find a replacement, and we hired an executive to replace me. My wife and I made a significant life change as we moved our family to London. I took three months to rest and recharge before starting our next GiANT company, GiANT Worldwide.

My Peace Index shot up immediately. My Purpose went from 60% to 93% by the end of that summer. The People were all working on the things that I was the most passionate about, Liberating People, which was high. We moved into an old manor house built in 1583 next to the River Thames on the edge of London, which made our Place majestic. My Personal Health climbed back without the amount of stress I had been experiencing for so long. The only issue was the Provision, which meant that I was paying for an expensive lifestyle and betting everything on the brand of GiANT for the future.

Steve Cockram played coach to me, and I coached him as we collectively began to build GiANT into a global business from a much healthier Peace Index. I think I climbed from 60% to an overall 93.5% that summer.

In the same way that every person has a number, they also have a driver. It is vital to understand the driver of those you live and work with, so you can help them improve their Peace Index as well.

Work on Your Lowest %

One of the Peace Index's benefits is that it tells you what area you need to focus on to improve.

If Purpose is the lowest, what can you do to reinvigorate your identity or meaning in your life and/or work?

If People are the lowest, what can you control in those key relationships to restore communication, relational trust, and alignment?

If Place is the lowest, can you move or change your home situation, living area, or office?

What can you do if Personal Health is the lowest to create a better regimen for your mind, body, and spirit?

If Provision is down, what can you control without scurrying out of fear?

I like how a client, Sophie Preston, put it: "If you're not serving the lowest indicator, it'll likely be draining the other indicators. Outflow determines inflow; take action in that area to reap the rewards."

To act, I suggest you improve your lowest area by working on making lists. Here is how to do that well.

1. List the area (Purpose, People, Place, Personal Health, or Provision) that is the lowest % and needs the most improvement. *People, Personal health*

2. Make a list of everything that is going right in that category. *Children - unpredictable menopausal*

3. Now make a list of everything that isn't going well in that category. *Children* *workout, eat right*

4. What is missing or needs to be improved upon specifically? *patience, continued prayer, more let go.*

5. Now make a list of what is confusing. What doesn't make sense?

After you brainstorm each list, you will have the information to improve the area. You will know how to boost what is going right in that category; fix what is not going well; add what is missing; and clarify what is confused.

Getting Results

Our business, GiANT, resources coaches and consultants worldwide to get results by unlocking people's potential and building better team leaders. We use over 70 tools like the Peace Index to do that. Here is one account from one of our team members, Chris Ediger, who is working inside a global company:

"I had a client who was working in an authoritarian culture at her company here in Atlanta. She was near the end of her rope when we introduced the Peace Index to the group. After the group coaching call, she sent me a spreadsheet she had created outlining her Peace Index in detail (listing out the current Peace Index scores for every significant person in her world at the time, etc.). When she compiled her scores, she was at a 48% on her overall Peace Index. Fast-forward six months and her Peace Index jumped to a 72%! From a 48% to a 72% in six months!

"The fantastic thing is that her situation had primarily remained the same from the first time she did the inventory. She was still in the same position at the same company facing challenges. She was still dealing with the same people who brought difficulty into her life. The difference was her mindset. Because she knew herself in the areas/people/things that were negatively affecting her Peace, she led herself in a way to not be impacted by them as much. Conversely, she was intentional in how and where she spent time and energy with the things bringing her Peace."

What Happens If You Can't Make Any Changes?

What could you control if you were working in healthcare during the pandemic? Not much. Your Purpose % could have quickly dropped while your People and Place scores had to be affected, too. All of these could have led to your Personal Health woes; all the while, any Provision increase most likely didn't make up for the loss of the other % numbers.

Several stories from numerous GiANT coaches working with healthcare clients stated that the overall Peace Index % numbers were in the low 40% range. That is dangerous. Unfortunately, reports of deep depression or worse have been rampant in the health profession as people were working to cope with the difficulties of a drop in their Purpose, People, Place, Personal Health, and Provision %.

One of the strengths of humans is adaptability and tenacity during challenging moments. We have heard dozens of stories of people beginning to build back even stronger amidst the dramatic period.

We can't control pandemics, wars, death, or personal disease, but we can control our insides (our minds and emotions). Internal Peace can exist when external chaos reigns.

In 2007, my wife and I were in an almost tragic accident as our taxi was hit by a drunk driver late at night in Cancun, Mexico, while we were in a hurricane. Talk about no control! We weren't driving but were in a taxi—in Mexico. And we were in the middle of a category 3 hurricane. My body was squashed as nine ribs snapped, my sternum expanded several inches in front of me, my intestines were severed, and I couldn't move my legs.

I had no control. And yet I was at Peace. We had just finished watching Mel Gibson in the movie *Signs*, giving up his faith because he lost his wife to a driving accident. As we jumped into the taxi en route to our hotel, I began to talk to myself and God with this prayer: "If anything happens to Kelly or our kids, I will trust you. I don't want to be like Mel Gibson. Oh, and if anything happens to me, I will trust you."

It was seconds later when my wife screamed to watch out as another taxi took us out as if it were a cruise missile. There was no external Peace as I shouted a death scream and was trapped in pain in that tiny Fiat, a sardine can–like taxi. However, I was internally at Peace because I had just had the conversation with myself and God. The movie prepped me for that prayer. I had no idea I would go on and see my life flash before my eyes as I saw the answer to my prayer, "Was I your man, God? Was I a good husband? Was I a good dad?"

The ending of life was happening just like people say it does. It was like a slide presentation of pictures and moments of my life that answered these questions. And it was happening in the chaos of high winds, sideways rain, and ambulance sirens. My inside, however, was calm as the eye of the hurricane. My wife looked at me with tears and confirmed my prayer without ever hearing me state it. She said, "I want you to know that you were God's man, a great husband, and an amazing dad." My Peace was complete. I closed my eyes and was gone.

I am still here. That story is in my first book, *Leadership Is Dead*. It simply points out that we can control certain things while being affected by others. Peace is an inside game, and the better we manage it, the better our lives turn out.

Peace can be found while everything crazy is around you.

Your Peace Plan

It is time for you to game plan your Peace. What will you do to improve or increase each area in the Peace Index? I would like you to review your notes in each chapter and highlight two to four items you would like to change or work on to improve your % per category:

Purpose:

- _____

- _____

- _____

- _____

People:

- _____

- _____

- _____

- _____

Place:

- _____

- _____

- _____

- _____

Personal Health:

- _____
- _____
- _____
- _____

Provision:

- _____
- _____
- _____
- _____

Now, take the top three or four overarching items that you will prioritize based on your findings.
Examples might be,

- "To increase my Peace Index, we will consider putting our house on the market to move closer to our kid's school for a better quality of life."
- "To increase my Peace of mind, I will add a more consistent morning workout routine to help me feel better and improve my Personal Health."
- "To improve our Provision %, I will review if I should take on the side hustle or not."

The Peace Index is a snapshot of a moment in your life. I want to encourage you to use the tool to set a baseline for your current reality and help you clarify your path to move toward 100%.

Year of Peace

Conquering the chaos can only occur when you trade up and build offensive systems to counter unrest. For me, it takes more than a book to make that happen. I need to start living differently, which can only occur when we begin to think differently.

If increasing your Peace is something you want to implement, consider a whole year of Peace. Imagine—365 days of restorative Peace! Here is how that can work in practical steps.

1. Finish this book and begin to implement the Peace Plan for you.
2. Share the details of your Peace Plan with someone close to you who is fighting for your highest possible good.
3. Choose a date on the calendar to start The Peace Index course.
4. Start The Peace Index course at www.thepeace indexbook.com to give you 60 to 90 days to establish healthy habits around Purpose, People, Place, Personal Health, and Provision. This course is interactive and will allow you to track your Peace Index and a

game plan your personal growth while you conquer the chaos in your life.

5. Potentially start a Peace Index group to hold yourself accountable during the process.

Let's stop the sabotage, conquer the chaos, and win the war of well-being as we seek Peace with ourselves.

The next chapter will show you how I have kept the Peace through a daily system. This process has changed the way that I live my life. It gives me what I need to conquer the chaos in my life.

CHAPTER EIGHT

Keeping the Peace

There is no one better than you to keep the Peace inside you.

There is no one else responsible for ensuring that you are at Peace other than you. Keeping the Peace is not your spouse's role, nor is it the role of your boss or best friend. You, and only you, can ensure that you have a peaceful mindset.

Keeping the Peace is a process. You can use systems and techniques to ensure you stay in the right frame of mind. Each person may do things a bit differently based on their personality wiring. I, for one, need a system even though I don't naturally love the monotony of daily rhythms.

I have found that the best leaders intentionally manage themselves and their Peace. They must know themselves to lead themselves well. Ideally, this self-leadership is a daily exercise.

To keep the Peace, I must be right in certain relationships. I am a feeler by nature, and I need to feel good about my relationship with God, my wife and kids, and business partners. If I am off in any of these, it affects other parts of my work. That is important for you to think about: What must be right for you to be at Peace?

In my past, I tended to store up frustrations and let them build up like a shaken-up soda bottle. Little emotions would gather and mix with more significant issues until the "straw that broke the camel's back" would explode like a volcano. My patient wife had to deal with my storing up of internal frustrations and not managing my emotions well. This process was like a form of sabotage as I didn't have a strategy for keeping the Peace.

I don't do that anymore. A few years ago, I began leading myself on the inside by managing my emotions, so they didn't become volatile; instead, I am making them work to my advantage. Here is what I do to keep the Peace inside of me daily.

1. Call-Up Session

I start my morning in Peace from the night before, which I will explain in-depth here.

When I wake up, the first thing I do is go to the mirror and give myself a look—I try to find myself. No, I don't look in the mirror and smile like the old *SNL* Stuart Smalley joke of saying to myself, "I feel healthy. I feel happy, and doggone it, people like me."

Instead, I try to catch myself from the daze of coming out of sleep and say something like, "Hey man, there you are. Let's go."

That starts a mental exercise process before my physical exercise called a Call-Up session. As I get dressed for my morning workout routine, I call myself up into my identity. I will get personal here and share some things that I say to myself. Please note that this is me and my own words to activate me early in the morning. You will have your own words and sayings that motivate you.

I usually say things like this: "Hey dude, it's time. Let's go. Wake up. Remember who you are. You are a liberator—a freedom fighter. You fight for the highest possible good in others. Let's go."

The process will wake up my mind and spirit as my body comes awake. After 50 years of living, I am finally finding out how to align my body with my mind, emotions, and spirit early in the morning. It's about time!

"When you make peace with yourself, you make peace with the world."
– Maha Ghosananda

At this point, I'm dressed and ready for the workout routine that my decathlete son, Will, helped me create in the garage gym. My Call-Up session lasts the entire workout. I usually have air buds in with either pump-up music or listening to some podcast as I continue to tell myself who I am, which is the core of Identity thinking. We must remind ourselves who we are.

Once I am fully alive, I begin telling God who He is to me today. Connecting like this brings me Peace as I feel aligned by the end of the workout. Again, this is my process, which could look different for you. The key here is to call yourself up and have alignment to feel connected with what is most important to you.

This process can take 15 to 45 minutes, depending on your schedule. It is not the length of time that matters; instead, it matters that you do it.

What motivational sentences, phrases, or bullets come to mind when thinking about your Call-Up session? What would inspire you to keep the Peace for yourself every day?

- Blessed & highly favored
- Daughter of the most High
- Glory days not gloomy days
- I can do All things through Christ
- Let Go & let God

Once I complete my workout session, I continue the Call-Up session as I shower and get dressed. I remind myself what I am doing that day and what superpowers I have to share.

When I turn the shower on, I start praying for "people of peace." I got this from reading about how Jesus changed the world when he taught his students what to do when they were going out into the villages to help people. He taught them how to look for "people of peace." If they found someone who wasn't, Jesus told them to shake the dust off their feet and move on, which is a great way to keep the Peace, by the way. It removes the chaos.

The morning Call-Up session does several things for me:

- It is a better way to wake up.
- It gets my mind in gear quicker.
- It reminds me of who I am.
- It gives me a way to connect with God, which I need to feel good about my day.
- It causes me to start thinking positively about the people I will meet that day.
- It is a system, and it feels good to complete it every day.

Many of you have mastered this through devotions or mindfulness, which may incorporate breathing techniques and meditation. I am just an average guy who has found something that fits me. I hope you will do the same in whatever works for you.

Does this sound like a lot of work? It can seem that way until you try your version of it. Here is the reality: you already have a morning routine but probably don't realize it. Why not make it better?

Most people wake up and check email or social media. When you do that, you allow other people to set your agenda when you are not ready to receive it. Why do that? Why let someone's writing or post from yesterday affect you when your mind is hazy and waking up?

If this is you, then you might move straight to the tasks at hand and begin to craft emails or phone calls. If you're not careful, this can lead to worry or anxiety, or frustration with the person you are responding to in your mind. This system is not productive or healthy. There is a better way.

Keeping your Peace requires you to start your mornings with intentionality. Peace requires work, and when you accidentally wake up in the mornings, you will receive the consequences of accidental living—messiness and drama.

Start tomorrow. Create a system that builds in some wake-up, motivational Call-Up comments to yourself that are not cheesy to you. Schedule some workout time with devotions or inspiration more critical than your to-do list. You will have time to get your list accomplished. You want to make sure you are as sharp and prepared as possible to deal with your tasks in the morning.

The Day

When you have set the Peace in the mornings, the day is more engaging and inspiring. You have more energy to do good work, more grace to give to others who could annoy you, and more perspective on what is essential and what isn't.

Get after it. Take ground in your job. Do good work. You know who you are and what you are about because you remind yourself in the morning and continue to call yourself up into that identity.

This process has taken me decades to begin to master. During my earlier years, I was prone to the emotional whims of others' comments. While I would start my day with devotions, I would quickly move into my task world with little Peace, which would lead to becoming emotionally up and down. This process led to inconsistency as a leader as some days were full of laughs and joy, while others were full of dread.

If you establish your morning in Peace, your days will be better because you train your mind to handle things in perspective. You become more secure and confident with who you are, and you know that the relationships you value the most are aligned in trust.

My morning routine is so helpful, but it is not enough. Yep, I said it. My morning Call-Up is not enough for me to keep the Peace every single day. I have learned that I had to add an afternoon process to help me stay self-aware and deal with any issues during the day.

2. The Examen

Every afternoon at 5:30 p.m., my alarm goes off to remind me that it is time for the Examen. The Examen has changed my life. Literally.

I did not create the Examen. It is an ancient reflective practice created by Ignatius of Loyola in 1522. As a Jesuit, he developed the method to help his followers improve discipline, increase self-awareness, and to become more aware of God in their lives.

Many are familiar with this reflective exercise and even use it daily. I have found that many don't, so I have adapted the Examen to fit my afternoon process. For the purists, please know that I value the complete Spiritual Exercises written by Ignatius. I have found something that fits my daily routine and modified it to fit my life.

When my 5:30 p.m. alarm rings, I immediately do the Examen in this format by asking myself these questions.

1. What am I grateful for today?

2. Where was I off (or on) today?

3. What do I need to be ready for tomorrow?

That's it. This process has changed my life. Why? Because it causes me not to allow emotions to build up over time, which I have a history of doing.

It is important to note that this process takes me anywhere between 5 and 15 minutes. I don't take notes or write in a journal. Instead, I contemplate the Examen wherever I am in the world—be it on an airplane, driving home, or running errands. My wife, Kelly, and I will even do the Examen if the alarm goes off while we are together. Also, I like to do this before dinner to clear my mind, and there is more Peace over dinner and the evening.

Phase One: Gratitude (1 to 3 minutes)

Try it right now. Ask yourself this question: What are you most grateful for today? It usually is between two and four specific and not general items. Don't overthink this. You could be thankful for a colleague or a successful meeting, your kids making good decisions, or a date night with someone special. You establish gratitude in your life, which leads to more health and Peace.

There are times when I will text someone my gratitude if I can, which makes that moment even more powerful. Either way, think about two to four things you are grateful for at the end of a long day and, where appropriate, tell someone.

Phase Two: Where Was I Off? (3 to 7 minutes)

Phase One takes a couple of minutes, especially as you get used to it. This next one, however, is much more difficult. It's difficult because you need to be vulnerable with yourself and willing to look in a mirror and see broccoli in your teeth.

Most days, we will have negative emotions or feelings toward someone or something. There might also be frustrations about a situation that causes you to react negatively. It is vital to have a trap to catch this negativity so it doesn't affect other people and so you can process it and deal with it appropriately.

Here is how it works. Ask yourself, "Where was I off today?" or "What didn't feel right?" Your mind will begin to package memories of the day to answer those questions. Examples might be "I didn't like how I responded to my wife. Why did I do that?" or "That conversation at work was so frustrating."

What you are not doing is finding a list of wrongs from others. The Apostle Paul writes, "If possible, as far as it depends on you, live at peace with everyone." The key here is "as far as it depends on you." That means it starts with us before we look at them. Looking inward is the secret of this section of the Examen.

I must state here a concern I have for some of you. If you tend to dominate yourself by bringing high challenge without high support, then this process could cause you to become even more harmful and dominating toward yourself. That used to be me.

I have focused on liberating myself by giving myself more grace while still holding myself to high standards for the last season of life. The Examen reinforces accountability without leading to shame or guilt. I am keeping short accounts with myself so that negatives won't stick to me. That could happen to you as you learn to keep the Peace through the Examen process. You must be willing for it to do its magic.

Here is a commonly asked question: What if someone did something today that was their fault, and it is real?

My usual process is to observe where I was off today, and I always start with me. If, however, I find that it was an issue with someone else and not with me, I then go to the source and address the issue directly. I use the Examen process to ask the question, come up with a solution if possible, and when and how I will manage them. If it is a challenge, I always deal with them face to face.

One other secret: I am learning to give them the benefit of the doubt. Not long ago, I had a situation come up with a business colleague, and during my Examen, I processed what felt off. I recognized one issue that was mine and two or three issues that seemed aggressive toward me. I immediately scheduled a call with my colleague, shared where I was off, and asked if we could process a couple of items. Two of the areas were simply misread, and one led to a more meaningful conversation about our communication in the future.

In my past life, I would have stored that up, keeping records of wrongs until too many moments had gotten pent up. Eventually, there would be a straw that broke the camel's back, and I would have hulked out in an awkward frustration.

"Where was I off today?" is a process of humility. It makes you more secure and confident as you get better each day.

One of my fun projects is working alongside Kevin DeShazo with the players and coaches on the University of Oklahoma football team. We are helping with sports performance and often share the concept of 1% improvement daily. When a player gets that, the quality of practice, school, and relationships goes up tremendously. This 1% every day adds up to a positive number at the end of a cycle.

The same is true for you. The Examen helps you work on the 1% improvement every day.

Phase Three: Preparing for Tomorrow (2 to 3 minutes)

Again, the entire Examen process takes me 6 to 15 minutes per day once I became proficient at it. The last stage of my version of the Examen is to review your next day, today.

What are you doing? Where are you going? What do you need to do now for tomorrow that you haven't already done? Who do you need to call, etc.?

Being prepared tactically is essential. Even more important is to be ready emotionally or relationally. To do that well, I will look at the calendar, think about the person, and try to walk a mile in their shoes. I will frequently also pray for the person or the situation to ensure that my intent and attitude are on target.

This section takes a few minutes and sometimes leads to a few more tasks either right then or that evening. What is encouraging is that this part of the process brings Peace in that I feel prepared and confident about the next day the night before. That allows me to enjoy my evening with far greater Peace than I have ever had before.

The Call-Up session in the morning and Examen session after work are fantastic ways to help me keep the Peace. However, over time, I have found that they are still not enough to help me keep the Peace needed in my life.

I recently added one last process for those evenings where some negativity or unrest made it through the filters I have created. It is a new exercise I am experimenting with as I sleep.

3. R.I.P. Sleep

R.I.P. might be a bit dramatic since it is a phrase mostly correlated to resting in the afterlife once someone has died. Rest in Peace is the goal here. I want you to sleep in Peace like you are dead (only not).

It is possible to sleep much better than you do. Most experts state you should shoot for seven hours of sleep per night. They are insinuating that those are good hours of sleep, which most do not experience because of pent-up emotions, frustrations from the day, and the pettiness that seems to stick to us and become enflamed in our minds when we try to sleep.

Each of us has a conscious and a sub-conscious. When we sleep, our conscious minds turn off and go to sleep, while our sub-conscious stays fully awake as we sleep. The sub-conscious is where dreams reside. Dr. Jarrod Spencer, who counseled me for years, shared that our minds are like computers, and at night they begin putting away the open files to reorganize the mind. If too many files are open or there is conflict occurring with others, the files will jam in the brain and cause a lack of sleep or more profound frustration.

Our subconscious is where all the pain and drama and negativity reside. That is why we must do the hard work of cleaning it out, keeping short accounts, and forgiving people. We must turn things off to turn on rest.

To keep short accounts and bring more Peace, I choose a theme every night and then wake up to it the very next morning. Some nights it is a phrase like, "Choose hope," or "Eradicate negativity," or "Worry is a prayer of disbelief. Stop the worry."

I then ask God to do the work on me while I sleep. It seems to make sense to me as a Maximizer. I have six to eight hours of sleep ahead of me. Why not ask God to work on me while I sleep? Why not allow my mind to reset for the next day with Peace?

This entire process may sound crazy to you. That's okay. How is your current sleep working for you? Sleep Peace works. Try it. Or create the process that will help you keep the Peace. Whatever it takes.

For me, I:

1. Call myself up in the morning to set the tone.
2. Do the Examen to ensure I am managing my emotions.
3. Engage Sleep Peace to make sure I am maximizing my rest.

Peace is available if you are available. Create the systems that allow you to eliminate the unrest to be a person of Peace to others. You will have conquered the chaos that keeps you from being your best when you do. You will have won the war for your well-being, a noble pursuit.

CHAPTER NINE

Taking Care of Your People

The previous chapters have focused on helping you win the war of your own well-being—to conquer the chaos that causes a lack of Peace.

This chapter is designed for people who lead others—an executive or boss, coach, or parent. It is for anyone who leads people or is responsible for taking care of others.

Through the years I have observed radical transformation inside people who finally got it. They woke up to the reality that they are responsible to help others get to the next level.

Taking Responsibility

Who are the People you are responsible for leading? To be responsible means having an obligation to do something or having control over or care for someone as part of one's job or role. That job could be a paid position like a team leader, manager, or executive. Or, that responsibility might be as the oldest child toward aging parents or simply your role as mother or father.

Leadership is responsibility. It means you take care of the people you lead. That is what leadership is. Leadership means you are 1) responsible for doing your own work (to perform) while 2) helping others do their roles (helping them perform).

When Steve Cockram and I wrote *The 100X Leader*, we highlighted the Sherpa on Mt. Everest as the best metaphor for leadership. The Sherpa must be the healthiest climber on the mountain while helping others climb. If they are not healthy, the climbers won't respect them or follow them. Because the Sherpa have a genetic predisposition to the altitude, they can climb higher and faster than most climbers. The climbers trust them because they are the healthiest and most experienced on the mountain.

In fact, our team at GiANT has created an Altitude Assessment that allows leaders to test themselves to see their level of trust and leadership with their People. The assessment highlights two numbers:

A. Your personal performance as a contributor (either at work or home). It gives you an option to assess how well you perform personally on a scale of 1 to 10.

B. Your leading other people. How well do you help others perform while you are performing? The assessment gives you an option of 1 to 10 as you honestly assess your ability to lead others.

You might give yourself an 8 out of 10 on how well you perform from a work perspective. As it relates to leading others, you might give yourself a 6, so you would be an 8–6. If you were to do the same assessment at home, you might state that you are a 7 out of 10 in your role at home and possibly a 6 in leading your kids/family. That would make you a 7–6 at home.

Once you recognize the power of this simple Altitude Assessment, you can begin to see your organization differently. How many employees do you have at your organization? How many team leaders do you have (people who lead people)? This list represents the number of Sherpa you have in your organization—the ones who are helping take your employees to the next level. I recommend drawing circles for the number of teams in your organization, putting the team leader's name in the middle of those circles, and then having them answer the Altitude Assessment for themselves while you also do it. Some might be an 8–4, while others could be a 6–7. Total up all the first numbers on their personal performance and divide by the number of team members. Do the same for the leading people numbers and see the average Altitude Performance of your Sherpa (your team leaders). This will show you what needs to happen to take them to the next level. You can take the Altitude Assessment for free at summit.giantos.com/store.

What does this have to do with the Peace Index? It means that your number needs to be the highest possible to have the influence and endurance to help others. If you have a low Peace Index while others have a higher number, you could drag others down. It could also affect the way you lead others. Conversely, if your Peace Index is balanced and you become healthier, you will have influenced others more consistently. Remember, no one wants to follow an unhealthy Sherpa up the mountain.

That puts the impetus on you to do all you can to be the healthiest to help others perform at higher levels while working on climbing at higher levels. If they don't see you as healthy or healthier than them, they won't want to respect your leadership in their life.

The Number

Remember the conversation about everyone having a number? Your employees walk in every day with a number over their heads. The number could be affected by heart palpitations the day before or from news of one of their children. It's true what they say: we are only as good as our weakest child! It is incredible how drama occurring in one or two circles can produce lower results, and you may have no idea why.

The same is true for our families. Every family member has a number over their head. Leading our families is more complicated because school and work can wear us out during the day, and the family tends to get the leftovers. That means that the numbers we experience when everyone gets home could be lower than at the start of the day. Keep that in mind as you lead your family.

Every person is impacted by the cause and effect of other people's decisions. When a child decides to fight the bully because they have had enough, it affects the parent employee of that child. When an employee's spouse chooses not to be healthy and needs special care, that affects you at work. Every action has a reaction. Every cause, an effect.

Smartphones and technology have only sped up this cycle. It is easier than ever to pass along frustration and drama through text messages, memes, and frustrating phone calls. That means we are aware of issues immediately anywhere we are. The old world of compartmentalization is gone. It is virtually impossible to separate work from home.

"Back in my day," says the old geezer, like me. We would leave school or go on a business trip with no email, text messages, or cell phone calls to affect us. Life moved differently than today, which affects how we lead. We are living in the digital age of 24/7 text cycles. Thankfully we aren't tracking sneezes in loved ones, but the technology can undoubtedly do that.

Improving the Number

So how do you help others increase their Peace Index number?

"How are you?" doesn't cut it. Everyone knows that game. The leader becomes a great leader by becoming a Sherpa for those they lead by asking them their Peace Index and working to help them, where appropriate, deal with the drama in their life, whether the unruly neighbor or the difficulty with Purpose.

A great leader, like the Sherpa, helps people; as my friend Kevin Weaver states in his book *Re_Orient*, "Contend for the highest possible good in every situation and relentlessly contend until it is a present-tense reality! with those you love."[1] Inside GiANT, we modified this to

---

[1]Weaver, K. (2013). *Re_Orient*. Oviedo, FL: Higherlife Development Services, Inc. https://thereorientbook.com.

state that a great leader "Fights for the highest possible good in the life of those you lead."

Fighting sounds strong until you understand that it means to bring high support and high challenge—to liberate people. You are a consistent freedom fighter for others for their highest best. And you stay in that role until it becomes a present reality.

Years ago, I had a solid team leader who began to pull away from me and others. My first couple of attempts of "How are you, really?" didn't yield anything. A frank conversation about what I saw in him, and his performance, led him to share that he and his wife were about to claim bankruptcy. I was shocked. He earned a good salary, and they seemed to live below their means; but however that happens, it was happening. They had credit card debt, and a counselor they were working with suggested bankruptcy so they could start over. In fact, he was filing in a couple of days.

This young man knew I was for him. I canceled my next couple of meetings, and we began to whiteboard his reality. I took this as a challenge; we created a game plan where he wouldn't need to declare bankruptcy. It would be a painful six months, but they did it. We would check in with each other over the weeks and months. I will never forget the hug and the celebration as one of my team members took control of his Provision issues and changed behaviors with his wife to overcome what was once impossible to resolve. Years later, we ran into each other at the airport, and we reminisced on the process and the freedom that came from fighting for what was right until it became real.

To lead well means your People (at work and home) know you care for them, not just yourself.

Leader Boundaries

Leaders are not licensed counselors, but they can counsel. I have had other moments in my leadership journey where deeper issues were at play, and I didn't realize it until later—divorce, abuse, mental health issues, etc.

A leader is not supposed to hold therapy sessions with their employees. That is why there are licensed professionals to ensure people receive the help they need to handle the complex issues in their life. Still, successful leaders can learn how to ascertain appropriate information to understand what is going on with their team members and help them overcome it to get to the next level, where applicable.

This is what liberation looks like—to help people achieve higher levels of Peace related to their Purpose, People, Place, Personal Health, or Provision. A great leader is a fighter—they take care of their People. This type of leader digs in just enough to know if the employee needs high support or high challenge and is adept at calling them higher to the level they should be.

Leaders are consistent helpers. They help people overcome their issues on the way to everyone becoming healthier. They even help train their teammates to teach others to become healthier.

This is what the world needs more of: selfless leaders fighting for the highest good of those they lead. If we had millions of these types of leaders inside teams and organizations and families, we would experience different levels of Peace worldwide.

Is that you? Is that your intent? If so, you are who I am called to serve. My Purpose is to raise up Liberators around the world—the freedom fighters we have been talking about. As a co-founder of GiANT, we have built certifications and systems to help scale these leaders inside every organization and equip coaches and consultants to bring Peace wherever they go. Liberation becomes a lifestyle that impacts every circle of influence in your life.

Conquering Chaos

Chaos is everywhere, but it doesn't have to be. It is your choice to either conquer it or allow it to reside in your mind, body, and spirit. It will cause you to go to war with the things set to destroy you.

Ronald Reagan was a fantastic uniter who wasn't afraid of a fight. He said it like this: "Peace is not absence of conflict; it is the ability to handle conflict by peaceful means."

There are external conflicts around every turn. It is the internal conflicts we are trying to tame. The Peace Index helps you know where you need to work on yourself. It is also a beautiful tool to help others grow.

The truth is that people are messy, full of chaos and unrest. They lead complex lives full of drama because of the cause-and-effect reality of actions and reactions. It is not your ultimate responsibility for their growth. They will want to grow to become healthier. For example, the Sherpa on Mt. Everest never carries anyone up the mountain. Your job is to call them up, show them how to build a game plan, and walk alongside them. If they choose to walk off the mountain, that is not your responsibility.

Your role is to be a healthy leader who fights for the highest possible good of the person you lead until it becomes a reality. Your job is to take care of your People.

Conclusion: It Is Up to You

"Nobody can bring you peace but yourself."
—Ralph Waldo Emerson

The Peace Index is a tool for you to use in your life from this time forward. It is visual so that you can remember it. It's simple enough for a 13-year-old and can be used in personal and professional relationships.

Tools are mirrors. When you look at them, you see things you want to improve. The common language allows you to be objective, not subjective. The tools don't lead to judgment but rather self-awareness.

The Peace Index allows you to see the pain, analyze it, and create a game plan for yourself while helping others do the same. It enables you to conquer chaos by witnessing it and creating a plan to resolve it.

Therefore, in conclusion, let me summarize what I would do if I were you with the content you have just learned.

Start by making a list of the unrest in your life. List what is not working. You might also list any anxieties or worries lodged in your mind. Examples of your possible dissatisfactions, fears, or unrest could be:

- My commute is miserable. I need to solve that.
- It feels like World War III could happen any day.
- My sister is driving me crazy. Something is off.
- Mark at work seems like he is against me.
- I feel that the political landscape could spill over into a civil war.
- I can't sleep. I wake up at 2 a.m. wide awake almost every night.
- My husband spends too much on frivolous things.
- I'm concerned we won't have the means to help our kids go to college.
- I am 40, and I still don't know what I am good at professionally.
- My son needs help. He can't focus on school, and it is becoming so hard for him/us to manage.
- My business partner and I are not on the same page, and our team is starting to feel it.
- Our country is heading in the wrong direction, and it worries me every day.
- We are renovating our kitchen, and it is taking so much longer because they found a leak. It is driving us crazy.

- I don't see how we can continue our lifestyle with my current salary. Something must give.
- My pants won't fit, and I will not buy a new wardrobe.

Some of these might fit you like a glove. I have found that making a list of dissatisfaction, fears, and concerns can be cathartic and helpful if you have a liberating mindset toward yourself—high support with high challenge. When you bring frustrations to light, you can begin to deal with them more openly.

1. Now go through the list, circle the ones you can control, and cross through those you can't control. We must separate worry from actual issues. We must dislodge worry from the center of our mind, body, and spirit. Anxieties create nothing good and rarely come true. Don't let them own you.

2. Since you have already taken the Peace Index, create a system to track it regularly. You can go old school and use Excel or make an air table (www.airtable.com) to follow your daily, weekly, or monthly Peace Index.

3. Make your game plan for each category, as mentioned in Chapter 7, Your Peace Plan.

4. Find your Driver and begin to observe and monitor it. If you improve that area, the entire Peace Index improves.

5. Work to implement Chapter 8, Keeping the Peace. I would love to hear success stories. Connect with me on Social Media platforms @jeremiekubicek.

6. Help others improve their Peace Index. Get them a copy of this book and have them join you on the Year of Peace.

7. Join me on my Peace Tour. Please invite me to your community or organization to speak and share the message. I will work to unlock people and make them stronger, more secure, and more confident leaders. Go to www.jeremiekubicek.com to sign up.

8. Finally, start the Year of Peace process with the course as the starter. Go to www.thepeaceindexbook.com.

Appendix

I have worked hard to understand my wiring and my Purpose. If you want to see what I am working on, here you go:

- Speaking/Coaching/Consulting: www. jeremiekubicek.com
- Certifications/Teams/Organizations: www. giantworldwide.com
- Intentional Parenting: www.sixsummers.com
- Sports Performance: www.culturewins.co
- Website Building: www.billion.me

If you like what you have read here and want to read my other works, visit Amazon.com.

Source: John Wiley & Sons

About the Author

Jeremie Kubicek is a prolific writer, speaker, and entrepreneur. He is married to Kelly and together they have three kids, Addison, Will, and Kate.

As a thought leader, Jeremie has created many books and resources:

Leadership Is Dead: How Influence Is Reviving It (*Wall Street Journal Best Seller*)

Making Your Leadership Come Alive: 7 Actions to Increase Your Influence (paperback update to *Leadership Is Dead*)

The 5 Gears: How to be Productive without Losing Relationships

The 5 Voices: What Is Your Leadership Voice?

The 100X Leader: How to Become Someone Worth Following

The Peace Index: A Five-Part Framework to Conquer Chaos and Find Fulfillment

He also co-founded GiANT Worldwide (www. giantworldwide.com) to serve coaches and consultants by giving them the tools, technology, and community to serve organizations globally.

He and his son, Will, have launched Six Summers to equip parents to help their 13- to 18-year-olds grow intentionally in mind, body and spirit. (www.sixsummers. com)

Along with Kevin DeShazo, he has built Culture Wins to help coaches and student athletes with mental performance and leadership. (www.culturewins.com)

Everything Jeremie works on is designed to empower people and create opportunities for them to grow.

He has lived in Moscow, Atlanta, and London, and currently resides in OKC with his wife, Kelly. They have co-developed a neighborhood and have built an event and wedding event center at their family farm outside of Oklahoma City.

You can find more out about Jeremie and his work at www.jeremiekubicek.com.

Index